CH00933138

THE CURRY BIBLE

THE CURRY BIBLE

Easy authentic recipes to make you go Mmmm...

This edition published by Parragon Books Ltd in 2013
LOVE FOOD is an imprint of Parragon Books Ltd

Parragon Books Ltd
Chartist House
15–17 Trim Street
Bath BA1 1HA, UK
www.parragon.com/lovefood

ISBN 978-1-4723-2342-2

Printed in China

Internal design by Talking Design
Introduction by Linda Doeser

Notes for the Reader
This book uses both metric and imperial measurements. Follow the same units of measurement throughout; do not mix metric and imperial. All spoon measurements are level: teaspoons are assumed to be 5 ml, and tablespoons are assumed to be 15 ml. Unless otherwise stated, milk is assumed to be full fat, eggs and individual vegetables are medium, and pepper is freshly ground black pepper. Unless otherwise stated, all root vegetables should be washed in plain water and peeled prior to using.

For best results, use a food thermometer when cooking meat and poultry – check the latest government guidelines for current advice.

Garnishes, decorations and serving suggestions are all optional and not necessarily included in the recipe ingredients or method.

The times given are an approximate guide only. Preparation times differ according to the techniques used by different people and the cooking times may also vary from those given. Optional ingredients, variations or serving suggestions have not been included in the time calculations.

Recipes using raw or very lightly cooked eggs should be avoided by infants, the elderly, pregnant women, convalescents and anyone suffering from an illness. Pregnant and breastfeeding women are advised to avoid eating peanuts and peanut products. Sufferers from nut allergies should be aware that some of the ready-made ingredients used in the recipes in this book may contain nuts. Always check the packaging before use.

Front cover recipe: Chicken Jalfrezi (page 58).

contents

introduction

Curry, derived from the Tamil word kari meaning sauce, has had a mixed history in the West. Employees of the Dutch East India Company and British colonialists returning home from India in the eighteenth and nineteenth centuries had developed a taste for the spicy sauces served with rice and other accompaniments during their time abroad. Unfortunately, attempts to re-create these subtly spiced dishes resulted in the use of commercial curry powder, something no Indian cook would or could have recognized.

Indian curry spices are traditionally prepared freshly for each dish and individual cooks have their own favourite recipes and adjust the mix according to the main ingredient of the dish. As well as dried spices, such as cumin and coriander, fresh ones, such as ginger and chillies, play an important role. None of these is just spooned into the pan, but carefully prepared first, often roasted or fried whole and then ground with a pestle and mortar. An extra spice mix may be fried in a separate pan towards the end of cooking and sprinkled over the finished dish before serving. Curries do not have to be hot, although some are, but must be aromatic and balanced. The range of spices used therefore is far more extensive than the list over the page and may include warm and fragrant flavourings rather than just hot ones.

Of course, curries also feature in the cuisines of other countries, especially in South-east Asia – Malaysia, Vietnam, Indonesia, Burma and Thailand. Although recipes vary from country to country, they often feature many of the same ingredients, such as coconut milk, limes, kaffir lime leaves, dried shrimp, fish sauce, galangal and fresh coriander. Thai curries are based on a curry paste, the best known being red, green and yellow. These are easy, if time-consuming, to make at home and many excellent commercial brands are available.

Nowadays, few Western cooks would even consider using curry powder and want to create a truly authentic flavour. The following recipes allow you to do just that, whether you want a creamy korma from northern India or a fiery Vindaloo from the south-west, a fragrant chicken curry from Thailand or a rich beef dish with a surprising kick from the original spice islands of Indonesia. A final chapter of recipes for accompaniments helps you add that finishing touch.

spices

Most curry spices are widely available from supermarkets and all can be purchased at Indian and Asian grocers. Store dried spices in a cool, dark, dry place and buy them in small quantities as they quickly lose their aroma.

Asafoetida: Obtained from the resinous gum of a tropical plant, asafoetida can be bought from Asian stores in block or powder form.

Cardamom: These green, cream or black pods are often used whole in savoury dishes, giving a slightly citrusy and eucalyptus flavour. They can also be broken open and the black seeds ground with other spices. Whole pods should be removed before serving.

Chillies: Both fresh and dried chillies are used in curries. There are many different kinds and it is difficult to tell how hot they are. As a rule, small pointed chillies tend to be hotter than larger, rounder ones. Thai or bird's eye chillies are particularly hot. Removing the seeds from fresh chillies also removes the membranes where most of the heat is concentrated. Wash your hands after handling chillies and don't touch your lips, eyes or other sensitive areas.

Cinnamon: This sweet, warm, fragrant spice is available ground and in sticks. Remove sticks before serving.

Coriander: It is best to buy these small beige seeds whole and grind them yourself, although ground coriander is available. This aromatic, sweet spice is widely used in both India and South-east Asia.

Cumin: Pungent and with a unique flavour, dark brown cumin seeds are often fried in oil, releasing a strong fragrance, before being ground. Ground cumin is also available.

Curry leaves: These aromatic leaves are used in the same way as bay leaves in Western cooking.

Fennel seeds: Smelling and tasting a little like aniseed, these are used to flavour Indian meat and vegetable curries. The roasted seeds are chewed to freshen the breath after a meal.

Fenugreek seeds: These small, tan seeds are very pungent and should be roasted before grinding with other spices. They are often used in Indian pickles and chutneys.

Galangal: A member of the ginger family and similar in flavour, it is widely used in South-east Asian cooking.

Garam masala: This hot, aromatic spice mixture is widely used in India and always added towards the end of cooking.

Ginger: The fresh root has a slightly sharp, clean taste. Peel off the skin with a sharp knife and chop finely. Ginger is often added to chutneys and pickles.

Kaffir limes: Not true limes, the fruits have a knobbly skin that is intensely aromatic when finely grated, but the flesh is inedible. Torn or shredded, the aromatic leaves are added to many Indonesian and Thai curries.

Lemon grass: Resembling a spring onion in appearance, these stalks have an aromatic lemony scent. It is widely used in South-east Asian curries, soups, curry pastes and pickles.

Mustard seeds: The fiery hot black seeds should be used with caution; yellow seeds are sweeter and milder. Add them to hot oil to release their flavour.

Saffron: The world's most expensive spice consists of the dried stigmas of a type of crocus. Only a small amount is required to flavour and colour rice.

Sesame seeds: These small, cream-coloured seeds have a nutty flavour and are used as a garnish and a flavouring for vegetable dishes.

Tamarind: The pods are dried to make a sticky pulp that must be soaked in hot water and strained before using. It has a very sour taste.

Turmeric: This bitter, bright yellow spice, available already ground, should be used sparingly.

thai red curry paste

- 1 tbsp coriander seeds
- 1 tbsp cumin seeds
- 2 tsp shrimp paste
- 12 dried or fresh red chillies, chopped
- 2 shallots, chopped
- 8 garlic cloves, chopped
- 2.5-cm/1-inch piece fresh galangal, chopped
- 2 lemon grass stalks (white part only), chopped
- 4 kaffir lime leaves, chopped
- 2 tbsp chopped fresh coriander root
- grated rind of 1 lime
- 1 tsp black peppercorns

Dry fry the coriander and cumin seeds in a frying pan, stirring constantly, for 2–3 minutes until browned. Remove from the heat and grind to a powder using a pestle and mortar. Wrap the shrimp paste in a piece of aluminium foil and grill or dry fry in a frying pan for 2–3 minutes, turning once or twice. Put the ground spices, shrimp paste and chillies in a food processor or blender and process until finely chopped. Add the remaining ingredients and process again to a smooth paste, scraping down the sides as necessary.

thai green curry paste

Follow the instructions for Thai Red Curry Paste, but replace the chillies with 15 fresh green Thai chillies, use only 6 garlic cloves, increase the number of kaffir lime leaves to 6, and add 1 teaspoon of salt with the pepper.

thai yellow curry paste

- 3 small fresh orange or yellow chillies, roughly chopped
- 3 large garlic cloves, roughly chopped
- 4 shallots, roughly chopped
- 3 tsp ground turmeric
- 1 tsp salt
- 12–15 black peppercorns
- 1 lemon grass stalk (white part only), roughly chopped
- 2.5-cm/1-inch piece fresh ginger, chopped

Put all the ingredients in a food processor or blender and process to a thick paste, scraping down the sides as necessary.

garlic & ginger paste

Blend together equal quantities of garlic and fresh ginger. Store in a sealed jar in the refrigerator for up to 3 weeks, or in a freezer for up to 1 month.

ghee

- 250 g/9 oz butter

Melt the butter in a large heavy-based saucepan over a medium heat until a thick foam appears on the surface. Continue simmering, uncovered, for 15 minutes, or until the foam separates, the milk solids settle on the bottom and the liquid becomes clear and golden. Line a sieve with a piece of muslin and place the sieve over a bowl. Slowly pour the liquid through the muslin, without disturbing the milk solids at the bottom of the pan. Discard the milk solids. Leave the ghee to cool, then transfer to a smaller container, cover and chill. Store in the refrigerator for up to 4 weeks.

masaman curry paste

- 4 large dried red chillies, stalks removed
- 2 tsp shrimp paste
- 3 shallots, finely chopped
- 3 garlic cloves, finely chopped
- 2.5-cm/1-inch piece fresh galangal, finely chopped
- 2 lemon grass stalks (white part only), finely chopped
- 2 cloves
- 1 tbsp coriander seeds
- 1 tbsp cumin seeds
- seeds from 3 green cardamon pods
- 1 tsp black peppercorns
- 1 tsp salt

Place the chillies in a bowl, cover with hot water and set aside to soak for 30–45 minutes. Wrap the shrimp paste in aluminium foil and grill or dry fry in a frying pan for 2–3 minutes, turning once or twice. Remove from the grill or frying pan. Dry fry the shallots, garlic, galangal, lemon grass, cloves, and coriander, cumin and cardamom seeds over a low heat, stirring frequently, for 3–4 minutes until lightly browned. Transfer to a food processor and process until finely ground. Add the chillies and their soaking liquid, peppercorns and salt and process again. Add the shrimp paste and process again to a smooth paste, scraping down the sides as necessary.

Mmmm...
meat

beef madras

serves 4

- 1–2 dried red chillies
- 2 tsp ground coriander
- 2 tsp ground turmeric
- 1 tsp black mustard seeds
- ½ tsp ground ginger
- ¼ tsp pepper
- 140 g/5 oz creamed coconut, grated, dissolved in 300 ml/10 fl oz boiling water
- 55 g/2 oz ghee or 4 tbsp vegetable oil or groundnut oil
- 2 onions, chopped
- 3 large garlic cloves, chopped
- 700 g/1 lb 9 oz lean stewing steak, trimmed and cut into 5-cm/2-inch cubes
- 250 ml/9 fl oz beef stock
- lemon juice
- salt
- poppadoms, to serve

1 Chop the chillies and put them in a small bowl with the coriander, turmeric, mustard seeds, ginger and pepper. Stir in a little of the dissolved creamed coconut to make a thin paste.

2 Heat a large frying pan with a tight-fitting lid or a flameproof casserole over a medium–high heat, then add the ghee. Add the onions and garlic and cook for 5–8 minutes, stirring frequently, until the onions are golden brown. Add the spice paste and stir for 2 minutes, or until you can smell the aromas.

3 Add the meat and stock and bring to the boil. Reduce the heat to its lowest level, cover tightly and simmer for 1½ hours, or until the beef is tender. Check occasionally that the meat isn't catching on the base of the pan and stir in a little extra water or stock, if necessary.

4 Uncover the pan and stir in the remaining dissolved coconut cream with the lemon juice and salt to taste. Bring to the boil, stirring, then reduce the heat again and simmer, still uncovered, until the sauce reduces slightly. Serve immediately with some poppadoms on the side.

balti beef

serves 4–6

- 25 g/1 oz ghee or 2 tbsp vegetable oil or groundnut oil
- 1 large onion, chopped
- 2 garlic cloves, crushed
- 2 large red peppers, deseeded and chopped
- 600 g/1 lb 5 oz boneless beef, such as sirloin, thinly sliced
- fresh coriander sprigs, to garnish
- naan bread, to serve

balti sauce

- 25 g/1 oz ghee or 2 tbsp vegetable oil or groundnut oil
- 2 large onions, chopped
- 1 tbsp Garlic and Ginger Paste (see page 11)
- 400 g/14 oz canned chopped tomatoes
- 1 tsp ground paprika
- ½ tsp ground turmeric
- ½ tsp ground cumin
- ½ tsp ground coriander
- ¼ tsp chilli powder
- ¼ tsp ground cardamom
- 1 bay leaf
- salt and pepper

1 To make the balti sauce, heat a wok over a medium–high heat, then add the ghee and melt. Add the onions and garlic and ginger paste and stir-fry for about 5 minutes until the onion is golden brown. Stir in the tomatoes, then add the paprika, turmeric, cumin, coriander, chilli powder, cardamom and bay leaf and salt and pepper to taste. Bring to the boil, stirring, then reduce the heat and simmer for 20 minutes, stirring occasionally.

2 Leave the sauce to cool slightly, then remove the bay leaf and pour the mixture into a food processor or blender and process to a smooth sauce.

3 Wipe out the wok and return it to a medium–high heat. Add the ghee and melt. Add the onion and garlic and stir-fry for 5–8 minutes until golden brown. Add the red peppers and continue stir-frying for 2 minutes.

4 Stir in the beef and continue stirring for 2 minutes until it starts to turn brown. Add the balti sauce and bring to the boil. Reduce the heat and simmer for 5 minutes, or until the sauce slightly reduces and the meat is tender. Adjust the seasoning, if necessary. Garnish with coriander sprigs and serve immediately with naan bread.

hot beef & coconut curry

serves 4

- 400 ml/14 fl oz coconut milk
- 2 tbsp Thai Red Curry Paste (see page 10)
- 2 garlic cloves, crushed
- 500 g/1 lb 2oz braising steak, cut into 2-cm/¾-inch chunks
- 2 fresh kaffir lime leaves, shredded
- 3 tbsp lime juice
- 2 tbsp Thai fish sauce
- 1 large fresh red chilli, deseeded and sliced
- ½ tsp ground turmeric
- 2 tbsp chopped fresh basil leaves
- 2 tbsp chopped coriander leaves
- salt and pepper
- shredded fresh coconut, to garnish
- freshly cooked rice, to serve

1 Place the coconut milk in a large saucepan and bring to the boil. Reduce the heat and simmer gently for 10 minutes, or until it has thickened. Stir in the curry paste and garlic and simmer for a further 5 minutes.

2 Add the beef to the pan and bring to the boil, stirring constantly. Reduce the heat and add the lime leaves, lime juice, fish sauce, chilli, turmeric and ½ teaspoon of salt.

3 Cover the pan and continue simmering for 20–25 minutes, or until the meat is tender, adding a little water if the sauce looks too dry.

4 Stir in the basil and coriander and season to taste with salt and pepper. Garnish with shredded coconut, and serve immediately with rice.

masaman curry

serves 4

- 2 tbsp groundnut oil or vegetable oil
- 225 g/8 oz shallots, roughly chopped
- 1 garlic clove, crushed
- 450 g/1 lb beef fillet, thickly sliced and then cut into 2.5-cm/1-inch cubes
- 2 tbsp Masaman Curry Paste (see page 11)
- 3 potatoes, cut into 2.5cm/ 1-inch cubes
- 400 ml/14 fl oz coconut milk
- 2 tbsp soy sauce
- 150 ml/5 fl oz beef stock
- 1 tsp palm sugar or soft light brown sugar
- 85 g/3 oz unsalted peanuts
- handful of fresh coriander, chopped
- cooked noodles, to serve

1 Heat a wok over a medium–high heat, then add the oil. Add the shallots and garlic and stir-fry for 1–2 minutes until soft. Add the beef and curry paste and stir-fry over a high heat for 2–3 minutes until browned all over. Add the potatoes, coconut milk, soy sauce, stock and sugar and bring gently to the boil, stirring occasionally. Reduce the heat and simmer for 8–10 minutes until the potatoes are tender.

2 Meanwhile, heat a separate wok over a medium–high heat, add the peanuts and cook, shaking the wok frequently, for 2–3 minutes until lightly browned. Add to the curry with the coriander and stir well. Serve hot with noodles.

beef korma with almonds

serves 6

- 300 ml/10 fl oz vegetable oil
- 3 onions, finely chopped
- 1 kg/2 lb 4 oz lean beef, cut into 5-cm/2-inch cubes
- 1½ tsp garam masala
- 1½ tsp ground coriander
- 1½ tsp finely chopped fresh ginger
- 1½ tsp crushed fresh garlic
- 1 tsp salt
- 150 ml/5 fl oz natural yogurt
- 2 whole cloves
- 3 green cardamom pods
- 4 black peppercorns
- 600 ml/1 pint water
- chapatis, to serve

to garnish

- chopped blanched almonds
- sliced fresh green chillies
- chopped fresh coriander

1 Heat the oil in a large, heavy-based frying pan. Add the onions and stir-fry for 8–10 minutes, until golden. Remove half of the onions and reserve.

2 Add the meat to the remaining onions in the frying pan and stir-fry for 5 minutes. Remove the frying pan from the heat.

3 Mix the garam masala, ground coriander, ginger, garlic, salt and yogurt together in a large bowl. Gradually add the meat to the yogurt and spice mixture and mix to coat the meat on all sides. Place the meat mixture in the frying pan, return to the heat, and stir-fry for 5–7 minutes, or until the mixture is nearly brown.

4 Add the cloves, cardamom pods and peppercorns. Add the water, reduce the heat, cover and simmer for 45–60 minutes. If the water has completely evaporated, but the meat is still not tender enough, add another 300 ml/10 fl oz water and cook for a further 10–15 minutes, stirring occasionally. Transfer to serving dishes and garnish with the reserved onions, chopped almonds, chillies and fresh coriander. Serve with chapatis.

coconut beef curry

serves 4

- 1 tbsp ground coriander
- 1 tbsp ground cumin
- 3 tbsp Masaman Curry Paste (see page 11)
- 150 ml/5 fl oz water
- 75 g/2¾ oz creamed coconut
- 450 g/1 lb beef fillet, cut into strips
- 400 ml/14 fl oz coconut milk
- 50 g/1¾ oz unsalted peanuts, finely chopped
- 2 tbsp fish sauce
- 1 tsp palm sugar or soft light brown sugar
- 4 kaffir lime leaves
- fresh coriander sprigs, to garnish
- cooked jasmine rice, to serve

1 Combine the coriander, cumin and curry paste in a bowl. Pour the water into a saucepan, add the creamed coconut and heat until it has dissolved. Add the curry paste mixture and simmer for 1 minute.

2 Add the beef and simmer for 6–8 minutes, then add the coconut milk, peanuts, fish sauce and sugar. Simmer gently for 15–20 minutes until the meat is tender.

3 Add the lime leaves and simmer for 1–2 minutes. Garnish with coriander sprigs and serve immediately with rice.

kheema matar

serves 4–6

- 25 g/1 oz ghee or 2 tbsp vegetable oil or groundnut oil
- 2 tsp cumin seeds
- 1 large onion, finely chopped
- 1 tbsp Garlic and Ginger Paste (see page 11)
- 2 bay leaves
- 2 tomatoes, deseeded and chopped
- 1 tsp ground coriander
- ¼–½ tsp chilli powder
- ¼ tsp ground turmeric
- pinch of sugar
- ½ tsp salt
- ½ tsp pepper
- 500 g/1 lb 2 oz lean minced beef or lamb
- 250 g/9 oz frozen peas, straight from the freezer

1 Heat a large frying pan with a tight-fitting lid or a flameproof casserole over a medium–high heat, then add the ghee. Add the cumin seeds and cook, stirring, for 30 seconds, or until they start to crackle.

2 Stir in the onion, garlic and ginger paste, and bay leaves and continue to stir-fry until the fat separates.

3 Stir in the tomatoes and cook for 1–2 minutes. Stir in the coriander, chilli powder, turmeric, sugar, salt and pepper and stir for 30 seconds.

4 Add the beef, using a wooden spoon to break it up, and cook for 5 minutes, or until the meat is no longer pink. Reduce the heat and simmer, stirring occasionally, for 10 minutes.

5 Add the peas and continue simmering for a further 10–15 minutes until the peas are thawed and hot. If there is too much liquid left in the pan, increase the heat and leave it to bubble for a few minutes until it reduces. Serve immediately.

lamb rogan josh

serves 4

- 350 ml/12 fl oz natural yogurt
- ½ tsp ground asafoetida, dissolved in 2 tbsp water
- 700 g/1 lb 9 oz boneless leg of lamb, trimmed and cut into 5-cm/2-inch cubes
- 2 tomatoes, deseeded and chopped
- 1 onion, chopped
- 25 g/1 oz ghee or 2 tbsp vegetable oil or groundnut oil
- 1½ tbsp Garlic and Ginger Paste (see page 11)
- 2 tbsp tomato purée
- 2 bay leaves
- 1 tbsp ground coriander
- ¼–1 tsp chilli powder, ideally Kashmiri chilli powder
- ½ tsp ground turmeric
- 1 tsp salt
- ½ tsp garam masala
- bay leaf, to garnish

1 Put the yogurt in a large, non-metallic bowl and stir in the dissolved asafoetida. Add the lamb and use your hands to rub in all the marinade, then set aside for 30 minutes.

2 Meanwhile, put the tomatoes and onion in a blender and process until blended.

3 Heat a large frying pan with a tight-fitting lid or a flameproof casserole over a medium heat, then add the ghee. Add the garlic and ginger paste and stir until the aromas are released. Stir in the tomato mixture, tomato purée, bay leaves, coriander, chilli powder and turmeric, reduce the heat to low and simmer, stirring occasionally, for 5–8 minutes.

4 Add the lamb and salt with any leftover marinade and stir for 2 minutes. Cover, reduce the heat to low and simmer, stirring occasionally, for 30 minutes. The lamb should give off enough moisture to prevent it catching on the base of the pan, but if the sauce looks too dry, stir in a little water.

5 Sprinkle with the garam masala, re-cover the pan and continue simmering for 15–20 minutes, or until the lamb is tender. Serve immediately, garnished with a bay leaf.

lamb pasanda

serves 4–6

- 600 g/1 lb 5 oz boneless shoulder or leg of lamb
- 2 tbsp Garlic and Ginger Paste (see page 11)
- 55 g/2 oz ghee or 4 tbsp vegetable oil or groundnut oil
- 3 large onions, chopped
- 1 fresh green chilli, deseeded and chopped
- 2 green cardamom pods, bruised
- 1 cinnamon stick, broken in half
- 2 tsp ground coriander
- 1 tsp ground cumin
- 1 tsp ground turmeric
- 250 ml/9 fl oz water
- 150 ml/5 fl oz double cream
- 4 tbsp ground almonds
- 1½ tsp salt
- 1 tsp garam masala
- paprika and toasted flaked almonds, to garnish

1 Cut the meat into thin slices, then place the slices between clingfilm and pound with a rolling pin or meat mallet. Put the lamb slices in a non-metallic bowl, add the garlic and ginger paste and rub the paste into the lamb. Cover and set aside in a cool place to marinate for 2 hours.

2 Heat a large frying pan with a tight-fitting lid over a medium–high heat, then add the ghee. Add the onions and chilli and cook, stirring frequently, for 5–8 minutes until the onions are golden brown.

3 Stir in the cardamom pods, cinnamon stick, coriander, cumin and turmeric and continue stirring for 2 minutes, or until the spices are aromatic.

4 Add the meat to the pan and cook, stirring occasionally, for about 5 minutes until it is brown on all sides and the fat begins to separate. Stir in the water and bring to the boil, still stirring. Reduce the heat to its lowest setting, cover the pan tightly and simmer for 40 minutes, or until the meat is tender.

5 When the lamb is tender, stir the cream and ground almonds together in a bowl. Beat in 6 tablespoons of the cooking liquid from the pan, then gradually beat this mixture back into the pan. Stir in the salt and garam masala. Simmer for a further 5 minutes, uncovered, stirring occasionally.

6 Garnish with paprika and toasted flaked almonds and serve immediately.

lamb & spinach curry

serves 2–4

- 300 ml/10 fl oz vegetable oil
- 2 onions, sliced
- ¼ bunch of fresh coriander
- 2 fresh green chillies, chopped
- 1½ tsp finely chopped fresh ginger
- 1½ tsp crushed fresh garlic
- 1 tsp chilli powder
- ½ tsp ground turmeric
- 450 g/1 lb lean lamb, cut into bite-sized chunks
- 1 tsp salt
- 1 kg/2 lb 4 oz fresh spinach, trimmed, washed and chopped
- 700 ml/1¼ pints water
- finely chopped fresh red chilli, to garnish

1 Heat the oil in a large, heavy-based frying pan. Add the onions and cook until light golden.

2 Add the fresh coriander and green chillies to the frying pan and stir-fry for 3–5 minutes. Reduce the heat and add the ginger, garlic, chilli powder and turmeric, stirring well.

3 Add the lamb to the frying pan and stir-fry for a further 5 minutes. Add the salt and the spinach and cook, stirring occasionally with a wooden spoon, for a further 3–5 minutes.

4 Add the water, stirring, and cook over a low heat, covered, for 45 minutes. Remove the lid and check the meat. If it is not tender, turn the meat over, increase the heat and cook, uncovered, until the surplus water has been absorbed. Stir-fry the mixture for a further 5–7 minutes.

5 Transfer the lamb and spinach mixture to a serving dish and garnish with chopped red chilli. Serve hot.

lamb, tomato & aubergine curry

serves 4

- 2 tbsp oil
- 500 g/1 lb 2 oz lamb fillet or leg, cut into 5-cm/2-inch cubes
- 1 large onion, roughly chopped
- 2–3 tbsp Thai Red Curry Paste (see page 10)
- 1 aubergine, cut into small cubes
- 10 tomatoes, peeled, deseeded and roughly chopped
- 400 ml/14 fl oz coconut milk
- 300 ml/10 fl oz lamb stock
- 2 tbsp chopped fresh coriander, plus extra sprigs to garnish

1 Heat the oil in a large frying pan. Add the lamb in batches and cook for 8–10 minutes, or until browned all over. Remove with a slotted spoon and reserve.

2 Add the onion to the frying pan and cook for 2–3 minutes, or until just softened. Add the curry paste and stir-fry for a further 2 minutes. Add the aubergine, three-quarters of the tomatoes and the lamb and stir together.

3 Add the coconut milk and stock and simmer gently for 30–40 minutes, until the lamb is tender and the curry has thickened.

4 Mix the remaining tomatoes and the chopped coriander together in a small bowl, then stir into the curry. Garnish with sprigs of coriander and serve immediately.

peshawar-style lamb curry

serves 4

- 4 tbsp sunflower oil
- 2.5-cm/1-inch piece cinnamon stick
- 5 green cardamom pods, bruised
- 5 cloves
- 2 bay leaves
- 700 g/1 lb 9 oz boneless leg of lamb, cut into 2.5-cm/ 1-inch cubes
- 1 large onion, finely chopped
- 2 tsp ginger purée
- 2 tsp garlic purée
- 1 tbsp tomato purée
- 1 tsp ground turmeric
- 1 tsp ground coriander
- 1 tsp ground cumin
- 125 g/4½ oz thick natural yogurt
- 2 tsp gram flour or cornflour
- ½–1 tsp chilli powder
- 150 ml/5 fl oz lukewarm water
- 1 tbsp chopped fresh mint leaves
- 2 tbsp chopped fresh coriander leaves
- naan bread, to serve

1 Heat a medium-sized saucepan over a low heat, then add the oil. Add the cinnamon, cardamom pods, cloves and bay leaves. Leave to sizzle for 25–30 seconds, then add the meat, increase the heat to medium–high and cook until the meat begins to brown and all the natural juices have evaporated.

2 Add the onion, ginger purée and garlic purée, cook for 5–6 minutes, stirring regularly, then add the tomato purée, turmeric, ground coriander and cumin. Continue to cook for 3–4 minutes.

3 Whisk together the yogurt, gram flour and chilli powder and add to the meat. Reduce the heat to low, add the water, cover and simmer, stirring to ensure that the sauce does not stick to the base of the pan, for 45–50 minutes, or until the meat is tender. Simmer, uncovered, to thicken the sauce to the desired consistency.

4 Stir in the fresh mint and coriander, remove from the heat and serve immediately with naan bread.

lamb in cinnamon & fenugreek sauce

serves 4

- 700 g/1 lb 9 oz boneless leg or neck end of lamb, cut into 2.5-cm/1-inch cubes
- 4 tbsp red wine vinegar
- 1 tsp salt, or to taste
- 4 tbsp sunflower oil
- 5-cm/2-inch piece cinnamon stick, halved
- 5 green cardamom pods, bruised
- 5 cloves
- 1 large onion, finely chopped
- 2 tsp ginger purée
- 2 tsp garlic purée
- 2 tsp ground cumin
- 1 tsp ground turmeric
- ½–1 tsp chilli powder
- 225 g/8 oz canned chopped tomatoes
- 1½ tbsp dried fenugreek leaves
- 175 ml/6 fl oz lukewarm water
- 2 tsp ghee or unsalted butter
- ½ tsp garam masala
- fresh coriander sprigs, to garnish
- cooked basmati rice, to serve

1 Put the meat in a non-metallic bowl and rub in the vinegar and salt. Set aside for 30–40 minutes.

2 Heat a medium-sized, heavy-based saucepan over a low heat, then add the oil. Add the cinnamon, cardamom pods and cloves. Let them sizzle for 25–30 seconds, then add the onion, increase the heat to medium and cook, stirring regularly, until the onion is soft but not brown.

3 Add the ginger purée and garlic purée and cook for a further 2–3 minutes, then add the cumin, turmeric and chilli powder. Cook for 1–2 minutes and add the tomatoes. Increase the heat slightly and continue to cook until the tomatoes are reduced to a paste-like consistency and the oil separates from the paste. Reduce the heat towards the end of the cooking time.

4 Add the meat, fenugreek leaves and water. Bring to the boil, reduce the heat to low, cover and simmer for 45–50 minutes, or until the meat is tender.

5 Heat a small saucepan over a low heat, then add the ghee. Stir in the garam masala. Cook for 30 seconds, then fold this spiced mixture into the curry. Remove from the heat, garnish with coriander sprigs and serve immediately with rice.

lamb do piaza

serves 4

- 4 onions, sliced into rings
- 3 garlic cloves, roughly chopped
- 2.5-cm/1-inch piece fresh ginger, grated
- 1 tsp ground coriander
- 1 tsp ground cumin
- 1 tsp chilli powder
- ½ tsp ground turmeric
- 1 tsp ground cinnamon
- 1 tsp garam masala
- 4 tbsp water
- 5 tbsp ghee or vegetable oil
- 600 g/1 lb 5 oz boneless lamb, cut into bite-sized chunks
- 6 tbsp natural yogurt
- salt and pepper
- fresh coriander leaves, to garnish
- freshly cooked rice, to serve

1 Put half of the onions into a food processor with the garlic, ginger, ground coriander, cumin, chilli powder, turmeric, cinnamon and garam masala. Add the water and process to a paste.

2 Heat 4 tablespoons of the ghee in a saucepan over a medium heat. Add the remaining onions and cook, stirring, for 3 minutes. Remove from the heat. Lift out the onions with a slotted spoon and set aside. Heat the remaining ghee in the pan over a high heat, add the lamb and cook, stirring, for 5 minutes. Lift out the meat and drain on kitchen paper.

3 Add the onion paste to the pan and cook over a medium heat, stirring, until the oil separates. Stir in the yogurt, season to taste with salt and pepper, return the lamb to the pan and stir well.

4 Bring the mixture gently to the boil, reduce the heat, cover and simmer for 25 minutes. Stir in the reserved onion rings and cook for a further 5 minutes. Remove from the heat, and garnish with coriander leaves. Serve immediately with freshly cooked rice.

mutton burra

makes 12

- 12 rib lamb chops, about 3.5 cm/1½ inches thick, with the meat of each chop sliced several times and the bones scraped
- vegetable oil, for brushing
- 40 g/1½ oz ghee or butter, melted
- chopped fresh coriander

tandoori marinade

- 300 g/10½ oz natural yogurt, strained through muslin for at least 2 hours, or 200 g/7 oz Greek-style yogurt
- 2 large garlic cloves, finely chopped
- ½ tbsp grated fresh ginger
- 1 tsp ground cinnamon
- 1 tsp ground cumin
- ½ tsp ground coriander
- ½ tsp cayenne pepper, or to taste
- pinch ground cloves
- pinch ground turmeric
- salt and pepper

1 To make the marinade, put all the ingredients, with some salt and pepper, into a polythene bag large enough to hold all the chops and mix together well. Add the ribs, seal the bag and leave to marinate for 4–24 hours.

2 When ready to cook, line a grill pan with foil and brush the rack with a little vegetable oil. Remove the chops from the marinade and wipe the ribs clean. Arrange the chops on the rack and drizzle with half the ghee.

3 Cook the chops for 10 minutes, then turn over and drizzle with the remaining ghee. Continue grilling for a further 8 minutes for medium or 10 minutes for well done. Leave to stand for at least 2 minutes, then sprinkle with coriander and serve. These can be served hot or cold.

pork with tamarind

serves 6

- 55 g/2 oz dried tamarind, roughly chopped
- 500 ml/18 fl oz boiling water
- 2 fresh green chillies, deseeded and roughly chopped
- 2 onions, roughly chopped
- 2 garlic cloves, roughly chopped
- 1 lemon grass stalk, bulb end roughly chopped
- 2 tbsp ghee or vegetable oil
- 1 tbsp ground coriander
- 1 tsp ground turmeric
- 1 tsp ground cardamom
- 1 tsp chilli powder
- 1 tsp ginger purée
- 1 cinnamon stick
- 1 kg/2 lb 4 oz diced pork fillet
- 1 tbsp chopped fresh coriander, plus extra sprigs to garnish
- sliced fresh red chillies, to garnish

1 Place the dried tamarind in a heatproof bowl, pour over the boiling water, mix well and leave to soak for 30 minutes.

2 Strain the soaking liquid through a sieve into a clean bowl, pressing down the pulp with the back of a wooden spoon. Discard the pulp. Pour 1 tablespoon of the tamarind liquid into a food processor and add the green chillies, onions, garlic and lemon grass and process until smooth.

3 Heat a large, heavy-based saucepan over a medium heat, then add the ghee. Add the chilli and onion paste, ground coriander, turmeric, cardamom, chilli powder, ginger purée and cinnamon stick and cook, stirring, for 2 minutes, or until the spices give off their aroma.

4 Add the pork and cook, stirring constantly, until lightly browned and well coated in the spice mixture. Pour in the remaining tamarind liquid, bring to the boil, then reduce the heat, cover and simmer for 30 minutes. Remove the lid from the pan and simmer for a further 30 minutes, or until the pork is tender. Stir in the chopped coriander and serve immediately, garnished with coriander sprigs and sliced red chillies.

pork vindaloo

serves 4–6

- 4 tbsp mustard oil
- 2 large onions, finely chopped
- 6 bay leaves
- 6 cloves
- 6 garlic cloves, chopped
- 3 green cardamom pods, lightly cracked
- ½ small fresh red chillies, chopped
- 2 tbsp ground cumin
- ½ tsp salt
- ½ tsp ground turmeric
- 2 tbsp cider vinegar
- 2 tbsp water
- 1 tbsp tomato purée
- 700 g/1 lb 9 oz boneless shoulder of pork, trimmed and cut into 5-cm/2-inch cubes

1 Put the mustard oil in a large frying pan or saucepan with a tight-fitting lid over a high heat until it smokes. Turn off the heat and leave the mustard oil to cool completely.

2 Reheat the oil over a medium–high heat. Add the onions and cook, stirring frequently, for 5–8 minutes until soft but not coloured.

3 Add the bay leaves, cloves, garlic, cardamom pods, chillies, cumin, salt, turmeric and 1 tablespoon of the vinegar to the onions and stir around. Stir in the water, then cover the pan and simmer for about 1 minute, or until the water is absorbed and the fat separates.

4 Dissolve the tomato purée in the remaining vinegar, then stir it into the pan. Add the pork and stir around.

5 Add just enough water to cover the pork and bring to the boil. Reduce the heat to its lowest level, cover the pan tightly and simmer for 40–60 minutes until the pork is tender.

6 If too much liquid remains in the pan when the pork is tender, use a slotted spoon to remove the pork from the pan and boil the liquid until it reduces to the required amount. Return the pork to the pan to heat through, then transfer to warmed dishes and serve.

railway pork & vegetables

serves 4–6

- 40 g/1½ oz ghee or 3 tbsp vegetable oil or groundnut oil
- 1 large onion, finely chopped
- 4 green cardamom pods
- 3 cloves
- 1 cinnamon stick
- 1 tbsp Garlic and Ginger Paste (see page 11)
- 2 tsp garam masala
- ¼–½ tsp chilli powder
- ½ tsp ground asafoetida
- 2 tsp salt
- 600 g/1 lb 5 oz lean minced pork
- 1 potato, scrubbed and cut into 5-mm/¼-inch dice
- 400 g/14 oz canned chopped tomatoes
- 125 ml/4 fl oz water
- 1 bay leaf
- 1 large carrot, coarsely grated

1 Heat a flameproof casserole or large frying pan with a tight-fitting lid over a medium heat, then add the ghee. Add the onion and cook, stirring occasionally, for 5–8 minutes until golden brown. Add the cardamom pods, cloves and cinnamon stick and cook, stirring, for 1 minute, or until you can smell the aromas.

2 Add the garlic and ginger paste, garam masala, chilli powder, asafoetida and salt and stir for a further minute. Add the pork, using a wooden spoon to break up the meat, and cook for 5 minutes, or until no longer pink.

3 Add the potato, tomatoes, water and bay leaf and bring to the boil, stirring. Reduce the heat to the lowest level, cover tightly and simmer for 15 minutes. Stir in the carrot and simmer for a further 5 minutes, or until the potato and carrot are tender. Taste and adjust the seasoning, if necessary, and serve immediately.

red curry pork with peppers

serves 4

- 2 tbsp vegetable or groundnut oil
- 1 onion, roughly chopped
- 2 garlic cloves, chopped
- 450 g/1 lb pork fillet, thickly sliced
- 1 red pepper, deseeded and cut into squares
- 175 g/6 oz mushrooms, quartered
- 2 tbsp Thai Red Curry Paste (see page 10)
- 115 g/4 oz creamed coconut, chopped
- 300 ml/10 fl oz pork or vegetable stock
- 2 tbsp Thai soy sauce
- 4 tomatoes, peeled, deseeded and chopped
- handful of fresh coriander, chopped

1 Heat the oil in a wok or large frying pan and cook the onion and garlic for 1–2 minutes, until they are softened but not browned.

2 Add the pork slices and stir-fry for 2–3 minutes until browned all over. Add the pepper, mushrooms and curry paste.

3 Dissolve the coconut in the stock and add to the wok with the soy sauce. Bring to the boil and simmer for 4–5 minutes until the liquid has reduced and thickened.

4 Add the tomatoes and coriander and cook for 1–2 minutes before serving.

burmese pork curry

serves 4

- 700 g/1 lb 9 oz boned leg of pork, trimmed and cut into 2.5-cm/1-inch cubes
- 2 tbsp dry white wine
- 1 tsp salt, or to taste
- 8 large garlic cloves, roughly chopped
- 5-cm/2-inch piece fresh ginger, roughly chopped
- 2 fresh red chillies, roughly chopped
- 1 large onion, roughly chopped
- 1 tsp ground turmeric
- ½–1 tsp chilli powder
- 3 tbsp groundnut oil
- 1 tbsp sesame oil
- 200 ml/7 fl oz lukewarm water
- 1 fresh green chilli, deseeded and cut into julienne strips, to garnish
- cooked basmati rice, to serve

1 Mix the meat, wine and salt in a non-metallic bowl and set aside for 1 hour.

2 Put the garlic, ginger, chillies and onion in a food processor or blender and blend until the ingredients are mushy. Transfer to a bowl and stir in the turmeric and chilli powder.

3 Heat the groundnut oil and sesame oil in a medium-sized, heavy-based saucepan over a medium heat, then add the puréed ingredients. Stir and cook for 5–6 minutes, reduce the heat to low and continue to cook for a further 8–10 minutes, sprinkling over a tablespoon of water from time to time to prevent the spices sticking to the base of the pan.

4 Add the marinated pork, increase the heat to medium–high and stir until the meat changes colour. Pour in the water and bring to the boil. Reduce the heat to low, cover and cook for 1 hour 10 minutes, stirring several times during the last 15–20 minutes of the cooking time to prevent the thickened sauce sticking to the base of the pan. Remove from the heat and garnish with the strips of chilli. Serve immediately with rice.

Mmmm...
poultry

chicken tikka masala

serves 4–6

- 400 g/14 oz canned chopped tomatoes
- 300 ml/10 fl oz double cream
- 1 cooked Tandoori Chicken (see page 90), cut into 8 pieces
- salt and pepper
- fresh chopped coriander, to garnish
- cooked basmati rice, to serve

tikka masala

- 25 g/1 oz ghee or 2 tbsp vegetable oil or groundnut oil
- 1 large garlic clove, finely chopped
- 1 fresh red chilli, deseeded and chopped
- 2 tsp ground cumin
- 2 tsp ground paprika
- ½ tsp salt
- pepper

1 To make the tikka masala, heat a large frying pan with a lid over a medium heat, then add the ghee. Add the garlic and chilli and stir-fry for 1 minute. Stir in the cumin, paprika, and salt and pepper to taste and continue stirring for about 30 seconds.

2 Stir the tomatoes and cream into the pan. Reduce the heat to low and leave to simmer for about 10 minutes, stirring frequently, until it reduces and thickens.

3 Meanwhile, remove all the bones and skin from the chicken pieces, then cut the meat into bite-sized pieces.

4 Adjust the seasoning of the sauce, if necessary. Add the chicken pieces to the pan, cover and leave to simmer for 3–5 minutes until the chicken is heated through. Garnish with coriander and serve immediately with rice.

chicken jalfrezi

serves 4

- ½ tsp cumin seeds
- ½ tsp coriander seeds
- 1 tsp mustard oil
- 3 tbsp vegetable oil
- 1 large onion, finely chopped
- 3 garlic cloves, crushed
- 1 tbsp tomato purée
- 2 tomatoes, peeled and chopped
- 1 tsp ground turmeric
- ½ tsp chilli powder
- ½ tsp garam masala
- 1 tsp red wine vinegar
- 1 small red pepper, deseeded and chopped
- 125 g/4½ oz frozen broad beans
- 500 g/1 lb 2 oz cooked chicken, chopped
- salt
- sprigs of fresh coriander, to garnish
- freshly cooked rice, to serve

1 Grind the cumin and coriander seeds in a mortar with a pestle, then reserve. Heat the mustard oil in a large, heavy-based frying pan over a high heat for 1 minute, or until it begins to smoke. Add the vegetable oil, reduce the heat and add the onion and garlic. Cook for 10 minutes, or until golden.

2 Add the tomato purée, tomatoes, turmeric, chilli powder, garam masala, vinegar and reserved ground cumin and coriander seeds to the frying pan. Stir the mixture until fragrant.

3 Add the red pepper and broad beans and stir for a further 2 minutes, or until the pepper is softened. Stir in the chicken, and season to taste with salt. Simmer gently for 6–8 minutes, or until the chicken is heated through and the beans are tender. Transfer to warmed serving bowls, garnish with sprigs of coriander and serve with freshly cooked rice.

green chicken curry

serves 4

- 2 tbsp groundnut or vegetable oil
- 4 spring onions, roughly chopped
- 2 tbsp Thai Green Curry Paste (see page 10)
- 700 ml/1¼ pints canned coconut milk
- 1 chicken stock cube
- 6 skinless chicken breasts, cut into 2.5-cm/1-inch cubes
- large handful of fresh coriander, chopped
- 1 tsp salt
- cooked rice, to serve

1 Heat the oil in a preheated wok, add the spring onions and stir-fry over a medium–high heat for 30 seconds, or until starting to soften.

2 Add the curry paste, coconut milk and stock cube and bring gently to the boil, stirring occasionally.

3 Add the chicken cubes, half the coriander and the salt and stir well. Reduce the heat and simmer gently for 8–10 minutes until the chicken is cooked through and tender.

4 Stir in the remaining coriander and serve immediately with rice.

chicken korma

serves 4

- 1 chicken, weighing 1.3 kg/3 lb
- 225 g/8 oz ghee or butter
- 3 onions, thinly sliced
- 1 garlic clove, crushed
- 2.5-cm/1-inch piece fresh ginger, grated
- 1 tsp mild chilli powder
- 1 tsp ground turmeric
- 1 tsp ground coriander
- ½ tsp ground cardamom
- ½ tsp ground cinnamon
- ½ tsp salt
- 1 tbsp gram flour
- 125 ml/4 fl oz milk
- 500 ml/18 fl oz double cream
- fresh coriander leaves, to garnish
- freshly cooked rice, to serve

1 Put the chicken into a large saucepan, cover with water and bring to the boil. Reduce the heat, cover and simmer for 30 minutes. Remove from the heat, lift out the chicken and set aside to cool. Reserve 125 ml/4 fl oz of the cooking liquid. Remove and discard the skin and bones. Cut the flesh into bite-sized pieces.

2 Heat the ghee in a large saucepan over a medium heat. Add the onions and garlic and cook, stirring, for 3 minutes, or until softened. Add the ginger, chilli powder, turmeric, ground coriander, cardamom, cinnamon and salt and cook for a further 5 minutes. Add the chicken and the reserved cooking liquid. Cook for 2 minutes.

3 Blend the flour with a little of the milk and add to the pan, then stir in the remaining milk. Bring to the boil, stirring, then reduce the heat, cover and simmer for 25 minutes. Stir in the cream, cover and simmer for a further 15 minutes.

4 Garnish with coriander leaves and serve with freshly cooked rice.

balti chicken

serves 6

- 3 tbsp ghee or vegetable oil
- 2 large onions, sliced
- 3 tomatoes, sliced
- ½ tsp kalonji seeds
- 4 black peppercorns
- 2 cardamom pods
- 1 cinnamon stick
- 1 tsp chilli powder
- 1 tsp garam masala
- 2 tsp Garlic and Ginger Paste (see page 11)
- 700 g/1 lb 9 oz skinless, boneless chicken breasts or thighs, diced
- 2 tbsp natural yogurt
- 2 tbsp chopped fresh coriander, plus extra sprigs to garnish
- 2 fresh green chillies, deseeded and finely chopped
- 2 tbsp lime juice
- salt

1 Heat the ghee in a large, heavy-based frying pan. Add the onions and cook over a low heat, stirring occasionally, for 10 minutes, or until golden. Add the tomatoes, kalonji seeds, peppercorns, cardamom pods, cinnamon stick, chilli powder, garam masala, and garlic and ginger paste, and season to taste with salt. Cook, stirring constantly, for 5 minutes.

2 Add the chicken and cook, stirring constantly, for 5 minutes, or until well coated in the spice paste. Stir in the yogurt. Cover and simmer, stirring occasionally, for 10 minutes.

3 Stir in the chopped coriander, chillies and lime juice. Transfer to a warmed serving dish, garnish with sprigs of coriander and serve immediately.

chicken in tomato & fenugreek sauce

Serves 4

- 700 g/1 lb 9 oz skinless, boneless chicken thighs, cut into 2.5-cm/1-inch cubes
- juice of 1 lime
- 1 tsp salt, or to taste
- 4 tbsp sunflower oil
- 1 large onion, finely chopped
- 2 tsp ginger purée
- 2 tsp garlic purée
- ½ tsp ground turmeric
- ½–1 tsp chilli powder
- 1 tbsp ground coriander
- 425 g/15 oz canned chopped tomatoes
- 125 ml/4 fl oz lukewarm water
- 1 tbsp dried fenugreek leaves
- ½ tsp garam masala
- 2 tbsp chopped fresh coriander leaves
- 2–4 fresh green chillies
- naan bread, to serve

1 Place the chicken in a non-metallic bowl and rub in the lime juice and salt. Cover and set aside for 30 minutes.

2 Heat a wok over a medium–high heat, then add the oil. Add the onion and stir-fry for 7–8 minutes until it begins to colour.

3 Add the ginger purée and garlic purée and continue to stir-fry for about a minute. Add the turmeric, chilli powder and ground coriander, then reduce the heat slightly and cook the spices for 25–30 seconds. Add half the tomatoes, stir-fry for 3–4 minutes, then add the remaining tomatoes. Continue to cook, stirring, until the tomato juice has evaporated and the oil separates from the spice paste and floats on the surface.

4 Add the chicken and increase the heat to high. Stir-fry for 4–5 minutes, then add the water, reduce the heat to medium–low and cook for 8–10 minutes, or until the sauce has thickened and the chicken is tender.

5 Add the fenugreek leaves, garam masala, half the coriander leaves and the chillies. Cook for 1–2 minutes, then remove from the heat and transfer to a serving plate. Garnish with the remaining coriander and serve immediately with naan bread.

butter chicken

serves 4–6

- 1 onion, chopped
- 1½ tbsp Garlic and Ginger Paste (see page 11)
- 400 g/14 oz canned chopped tomatoes
- ¼–½ tsp chilli powder
- pinch of sugar
- 30 g/1 oz ghee or 2 tbsp vegetable or groundnut oil
- 125 ml/4 fl oz water
- 1 tbsp tomato purée
- 40 g/1½ oz butter, cut into small pieces
- ½ tsp garam masala
- ½ tsp ground cumin
- ½ tsp ground coriander
- 8 cooked tandoori chicken pieces
- 4 tbsp double cream
- salt and pepper
- chopped cashew nuts and fresh coriander sprigs, to garnish

1 Put the onion and garlic and ginger paste in a food processor or blender and process until a paste forms. Add the tomatoes, chilli powder, sugar and a pinch of salt and process again until blended.

2 Melt the ghee in a wok or large frying pan over a medium–high heat. Add the tomato mixture and water and stir in the tomato pureé.

3 Bring the mixture to the boil, stirring, then reduce the heat to low and simmer for 5 minutes, stirring occasionally, until the sauce thickens.

4 Stir in half the butter, the garam masala, cumin and coriander. Add the chicken pieces and stir around until they are well coated. Simmer for a further 10 minutes, or until the chicken is hot. Taste and adjust the seasoning, if necessary.

5 Lightly beat the cream in a small bowl and stir in several tablespoons of the hot sauce, beating constantly. Stir the cream mixture into the tomato sauce, then add the remaining butter and stir until it melts. Garnish with the chopped cashew nuts and coriander sprigs and serve straight from the pan.

sri lankan chicken curry

serves 4

- 700 g/1 lb 9 oz skinless, boneless chicken thighs or breasts
- 1 tsp salt, or to taste
- 2 tbsp white wine vinegar
- 2 tsp coriander seeds
- 1 tsp cumin seeds
- 2.5-cm/1-inch piece cinnamon stick, broken up
- 4 cloves
- 4 green cardamom pods
- 6 fenugreek seeds
- 4 dried red chillies, torn into pieces
- 10–12 curry leaves
- 4 tbsp sunflower oil
- 1 large onion, finely chopped
- 2 tsp ginger purée
- 2 tsp garlic purée
- 1 tsp ground turmeric
- ½ tsp chilli powder
- 1 lemon grass stalk, finely sliced
- 200 g/7 oz canned chopped tomatoes
- 150 ml/5 fl oz lukewarm water
- 55 g/2 oz creamed coconut, cut into small pieces
- cooked basmati rice, to serve

1 Cut the chicken into 5-cm/2-inch chunks and put them in a non-metallic bowl. Add the salt and vinegar, mix well and set aside for 30 minutes.

2 Heat a small, heavy-based saucepan over a medium heat, then add the coriander seeds, cumin seeds, cinnamon, cloves, cardamom pods, fenugreek, chillies and curry leaves and dry-roast until they are dark, but not black. Remove and leave to cool, then grind in a spice grinder until finely ground. Set aside.

3 Heat a wok over a medium heat, then add the oil. Add the onion and cook for 5 minutes until translucent. Add the ginger purée and garlic purée and continue to cook for a further 2 minutes.

4 Add the turmeric, chilli powder, chicken and the ground spice mix. Stir and mix well, then add the lemon grass, tomatoes and water. Bring to the boil, reduce the heat to low, cover the wok and cook for 25 minutes.

5 Add the coconut and stir until it has dissolved. Cook for 7–8 minutes, then remove from the heat and serve immediately with rice.

thai red chicken curry

serves 2 -4

- 6 garlic cloves, chopped
- 2 red chillies, chopped
- 2 tbsp chopped lemon grass
- 1 tsp finely grated lime rind
- 1 tbsp chopped lime leaves
- 1 tbsp Thai Red Curry Paste (see page 10)
- 1 tbsp coriander seeds
- 1 tbsp chilli oil
- 4 skinless, boneless chicken breasts, sliced
- 300 ml/10 fl oz coconut milk
- 300 ml/10 fl oz chicken stock
- 1 tbsp soy sauce
- 55 g/2 oz ground peanuts
- 3 spring onions, sliced
- 1 red pepper, deseeded and sliced
- 3 Thai aubergines, sliced
- chopped fresh coriander,
- to garnish
- cooked rice, to serve

1 Place the garlic, chillies, lemon grass, lime rind, lime leaves, curry paste and coriander seeds in a food processor and process until the mixture is smooth.

2 Heat the oil in a preheated wok or large frying pan over a high heat. Add the chicken and the garlic mixture and stir-fry for 5 minutes. Add the coconut milk, stock and soy sauce and bring to the boil. Reduce the heat and cook, stirring, for a further 3 minutes. Stir in the ground peanuts and simmer for 20 minutes.

3 Add the spring onions, red pepper and aubergines and leave to simmer, stirring occasionally, for a further 10 minutes. Garnish with coriander and serve with cooked rice.

fried chilli chicken

serves 4

- 750 g/1 lb 10 oz chicken thighs
- 3 tbsp lemon juice
- 1 tsp salt, or to taste
- 5 large garlic cloves, roughly chopped
- 5-cm/2-inch piece fresh ginger, roughly chopped
- 1 medium onion, roughly chopped
- 2 fresh red chillies, roughly chopped
- 4 tbsp groundnut oil
- 1 tsp ground turmeric
- ½ tsp chilli powder
- 150 ml/5 fl oz lukewarm water
- 3–4 fresh green chillies
- cooked basmati rice, to serve

1 Put the chicken in a non-metallic bowl and rub in the lemon juice and salt. Set aside for 30 minutes.

2 Meanwhile, purée the garlic, ginger, onion and red chillies in a food processor or blender. Add a little water, if necessary, to facilitate blade movement if using a blender.

3 Heat a wide, shallow saucepan, preferably non-stick, over a medium–high heat, then add the oil. When the oil is hot, add the chicken in two batches and cook until golden brown on all sides. Lift out of the pan and drain on kitchen paper.

4 Add the puréed ingredients to the pan with the turmeric and chilli powder and reduce the heat to medium. Cook for 5–6 minutes, stirring regularly.

5 Add the chicken and water. Bring to the boil, reduce the heat to low, cover and cook for 20 minutes. Increase the heat to medium and cook for a further 8–10 minutes, stirring halfway through to ensure that the thickened sauce does not stick to the base of the pan.

6 Remove the lid and cook until the sauce is reduced to a paste-like consistency, stirring regularly to prevent the sauce sticking to the base of the pan. Add the green chillies and cook for 2–3 minutes, then remove from the heat and serve immediately with rice.

vietnamese chicken curry

serves 6

- 2 lemon grass stalks
- 50 ml/2 fl oz vegetable oil
- 3 large garlic cloves, crushed
- 1 large shallot, thinly sliced
- 2 tbsp Indian curry powder
- 700 ml/1¼ pints coconut milk
- 500 ml/18 fl oz coconut water (not coconut milk) or chicken stock
- 2 tbsp fish sauce
- 4 fresh red bird's eye chillies or dried red Chinese (tien sien) chillies
- 6 kaffir lime leaves
- 6 boneless chicken thighs or breasts, 175–225 g/6–8 oz each, with or without skin, cut into 5-cm/2-inch pieces
- 1 large white yam or sweet potato, peeled and cut into 2.5-cm/1-inch chunks
- 2 Asian aubergines, cut into 2.5-cm/1-inch pieces
- 250 g/9 oz French beans, topped and tailed
- 2 carrots, peeled and cut diagonally into 1 cm/½ inch thick pieces
- fresh Thai basil sprigs, to garnish
- cooked jasmine rice, to serve

1 Discard the bruised leaves and root ends of the lemon grass stalks, then cut 15–20 cm/6–8 inches of the lower stalks into paper-thin slices.

2 Heat a wok over a high heat, then add the oil. Add the garlic and shallot and stir-fry for 5 minutes, or until golden. Add the lemon grass and curry powder and stir-fry for 2 minutes, or until fragrant. Add the coconut milk, coconut water, fish sauce, chillies and lime leaves and bring to the boil.

3 Reduce the heat to low and add the chicken, yam, aubergines, beans and carrots. Simmer, covered, for 1 hour, or until the chicken and vegetables are tender and the flavours have blended.

4 Serve immediately, garnished with Thai basil sprigs and accompanied by jasmine rice.

chicken breasts with coconut milk

serves 4

- 1 small onion, chopped
- 1 fresh green chilli, deseeded and chopped
- 2.5-cm/1-inch piece fresh ginger, chopped
- 2 tsp ground coriander
- 1 tsp ground cumin
- 1 tsp fennel seeds
- 1 tsp ground star anise
- 1 tsp cardamom pods
- ½ tsp ground turmeric
- ½ tsp black peppercorns
- ½ tsp ground cloves
- 600 ml/1 pint canned coconut milk
- 4 skinless, boneless chicken breast portions
- vegetable oil, for brushing
- fresh coriander sprigs, to garnish

1 Place the onion, chilli, ginger, ground coriander, cumin, fennel seeds, star anise, cardamom pods, turmeric, peppercorns, cloves and 450 ml/16 fl oz of the coconut milk in a food processor and process to make a paste, adding more coconut milk if necessary.

2 Using a sharp knife, slash the chicken breasts several times and place in a large, shallow, non-metallic dish in a single layer. Pour over half the coconut milk mixture and turn to coat completely. Cover with clingfilm and leave to marinate in the refrigerator for at least 1 hour and up to 8 hours.

3 Heat a ridged griddle pan, then brush lightly with vegetable oil. Add the chicken, in batches if necessary, and cook for 6–7 minutes on each side, or until tender.

4 Meanwhile, pour the remaining coconut milk mixture into a saucepan and bring to the boil, stirring occasionally. Arrange the chicken on a warmed serving dish, spoon over a little of the coconut sauce and garnish with coriander sprigs. Serve hot.

shredded chicken & mixed mushrooms

serves 4–6

- 2 tbsp vegetable oil or groundnut oil
- 2 skinless, boneless chicken breasts
- 1 red onion, sliced
- 2 garlic cloves, finely chopped
- 2.5-cm/1-inch piece fresh ginger, grated
- 115 g/4 oz baby button mushrooms
- 115 g/4 oz shiitake mushrooms, halved
- 115 g/4 oz chestnut mushrooms, sliced
- 2–3 tbsp Thai Green Curry Paste (see page 10)
- 2 tbsp Thai soy sauce
- 4 tbsp chopped fresh parsley
- cooked noodles, to serve

1 Heat a wok over a medium heat, then add the oil. Add the chicken and cook on all sides until lightly browned and cooked through. Remove with a slotted spoon, shred into even-sized pieces and set aside.

2 Pour off any excess oil, then add the onion, garlic and ginger and stir-fry for 1–2 minutes until soft. Add the mushrooms and stir-fry for 2–3 minutes until they start to brown.

3 Add the curry paste, soy sauce and shredded chicken to the wok and stir-fry for 1–2 minutes. Stir in the parsley and serve immediately with noodles.

creamy chicken curry with spinach

serves 4

- 25 g/1 oz butter
- 4 tbsp olive oil
- 1 onion, finely chopped
- 2 garlic cloves, finely chopped
- 1 tbsp chopped fresh ginger
- 1 fresh green chilli, deseeded and chopped
- 1 celery stick, finely chopped
- 400 g/14 oz canned chopped tomatoes
- 2 tbsp tomato purée
- brown sugar, to taste
- ½ tsp ground cumin
- ½ tsp ground coriander
- ½ tsp ground turmeric
- ¼ tsp garam masala
- 100 ml/3½ fl oz water
- 600 g/1 lb 5 oz diced chicken
- 150 ml/5 fl oz double cream
- 200 g/7 oz baby spinach
- salt and pepper
- warm naan bread, to serve

1 Melt the butter with half the oil in a saucepan. Add the onion, garlic, ginger, chilli and celery and cook over a low heat, stirring occasionally, for 5 minutes, until softened. Stir in the tomatoes, tomato purée, sugar to taste, spices and water and season to taste with salt and pepper. Increase the heat to medium and bring to the boil, then reduce the heat and simmer, stirring occasionally, for 15–20 minutes, until thickened.

2 Meanwhile, heat the remaining oil in a frying pan. Add the chicken and cook over a medium heat, stirring frequently, for 5–7 minutes, until lightly browned all over. Remove with a slotted spoon.

3 Stir the chicken and cream into the sauce and simmer for 6 minutes, until the meat is tender and cooked through. Add the spinach and cook, stirring constantly, for 2–4 minutes, until wilted. Bring back to the boil, then transfer to a warmed serving dish. Serve immediately with naan bread.

thai yellow chicken curry

serves 4

- 2 tbsp vegetable oil or groundnut oil
- 2 onions, cut into thin wedges
- 2 garlic cloves, finely chopped
- 2 skinless, boneless chicken breasts, cut into strips
- 175 g/6 oz baby corn, halved lengthways

spice paste

- 6 tbsp Thai Yellow Curry Paste (see page 10)
- 150 ml/5 fl oz natural yogurt
- 400 ml/14 fl oz water
- handful of fresh coriander, chopped
- handful of fresh Thai basil leaves, shredded, plus extra sprigs to garnish

1 To make the spice paste, heat a wok over a medium heat, then add the curry paste and stir-fry for 2–3 minutes. Stir in the yogurt, water and herbs, bring to the boil and simmer for 2–3 minutes.

2 Meanwhile, heat a separate wok over a medium–high heat, then add the oil. Add the onions and garlic and stir-fry for 2–3 minutes. Add the chicken and corn and stir-fry for 3–4 minutes until the meat and corn are tender.

3 Stir in the spice paste and bring to the boil. Simmer for 2–3 minutes until heated through. Serve immediately, garnished with basil sprigs.

chicken & peanut curry

serves 4

- 1 tbsp vegetable oil or groundnut oil
- 2 red onions, sliced
- 2 tbsp Penang Curry Paste.
- 400 ml/14 fl oz coconut milk
- 150 ml/5 fl oz chicken stock
- 4 kaffir lime leaves, roughly torn
- 1 lemon grass stem, finely chopped
- 6 skinless, boneless chicken thighs, chopped
- 1 tbsp Thai fish sauce
- 2 tbsp Thai soy sauce
- 1 tsp palm sugar or soft light brown sugar
- 50 g/1¾ oz unsalted roasted peanuts, chopped, plus extra to serve
- 175 g/6 oz fresh pineapple, roughly chopped
- 15-cm/6-inch piece cucumber, peeled, deseeded and thickly sliced, plus extra to serve

1 Heat a wok over a medium–high heat, then add the oil. Add the onions and stir-fry for 1 minute. Add the curry paste and stir-fry for 1–2 minutes.

2 Pour in the coconut milk and stock. Add the lime leaves and lemon grass and simmer for 1 minute. Add the chicken and gradually bring to the boil. Simmer for 8–10 minutes until the chicken is tender.

3 Stir in the fish sauce, soy sauce and sugar and simmer for 1–2 minutes. Stir in the peanuts, pineapple and cucumber and cook for 30 seconds. Serve immediately with peanuts and cucumber on top.

cumin-scented chicken curry

serves 4

- 700 g/1 lb 9 oz boneless chicken thighs or breasts, cut into 5-cm/2-inch pieces
- juice of 1 lime
- 1 tsp salt, or to taste
- 3 tbsp sunflower oil
- 1 tsp cumin seeds
- 2.5-cm/1-inch piece cinnamon stick
- 5 green cardamom pods, bruised
- 4 cloves
- 1 large onion, finely chopped
- 2 tsp garlic purée
- 2 tsp ginger purée
- ½ tsp ground turmeric
- 2 tsp ground cumin
- ½ tsp chilli powder
- 225 g/8 oz canned chopped tomatoes
- 1 tbsp tomato purée
- ½ tsp sugar
- 225 ml/8 fl oz lukewarm water
- ½ tsp garam masala
- 2 tbsp chopped fresh coriander leaves, plus extra sprigs to garnish
- naan bread, to serve

1 Put the chicken in a non-metallic bowl and rub in the lime juice and salt. Cover and set aside for 30 minutes.

2 Heat a wok over a low heat, then add the oil. Add the cumin seeds, cinnamon, cardamom pods and cloves. Leave them to sizzle for 25–30 seconds, then add the onion. Cook, stirring frequently, for 5 minutes, or until the onion is soft.

3 Add the garlic purée and ginger purée and cook for about a minute, then add the turmeric, ground cumin and chilli powder. Add the tomatoes, tomato purée and sugar. Cook over a medium heat, stirring regularly, until the tomatoes reach a paste-like consistency and the oil separates from the paste. Sprinkle over a little water if the mixture sticks to the wok.

4 Add the chicken and increase the heat to medium–high. Stir until the chicken changes colour, then pour in the water. Bring to the boil, reduce the heat to medium–low and cook for 12–15 minutes, or until the sauce has thickened and the chicken is tender.

5 Stir in the garam masala and chopped coriander. Transfer to a serving dish and garnish with coriander sprigs. Serve immediately with naan bread.

tandoori chicken

serves 4

- 1 chicken, weighing 1.5 kg/3 lb 5 oz, skinned
- ½ lemon
- 1 tsp salt
- 25 g/1 oz ghee, melted
- fresh coriander sprigs, to garnish
- cooked basmati rice and lemon wedges, to serve

tandoori masala paste

- 1 tbsp Garlic and Ginger Paste (see page 11)
- 1 tbsp ground paprika
- 1 tsp ground cinnamon
- 1 tsp ground cumin
- ½ tsp ground coriander
- ¼ tsp chilli powder, ideally Kashmiri chilli powder
- pinch of ground cloves
- ¼ tsp red food colouring (optional)
- few drops of yellow food colouring (optional)
- 200 ml/7 fl oz natural yogurt

1 To make the tandoori masala paste, combine the garlic and ginger paste, dry spices and food colouring, if using, in a bowl and stir in the yogurt. The paste can be used immediately or stored in an airtight container in the refrigerator for up to 3 days.

2 Use a small knife to make thin cuts all over the chicken. Rub the lemon half over the chicken, then rub the salt into the cuts. Put the chicken in a deep, non-metallic bowl, add the paste and use your hands to rub it all over the bird and into the cuts. Cover the bowl with clingfilm and refrigerate for at least 4 hours, but ideally up to 24 hours.

3 When you are ready to cook the chicken, preheat the oven to 200°C/400°F/Gas Mark 6. Put the chicken on a rack in a roasting tin, breast-side up, and drizzle over the melted ghee. Roast in the preheated oven for 45 minutes, then quickly remove the bird from the oven in the tin and increase the temperature to its highest setting.

4 Very carefully pour out any fat from the bottom of the tin. Return the chicken to the oven and roast for a further 10–15 minutes until the juices run clear when you pierce the thigh with a knife and the paste is lightly charred.

5 Leave to stand for 10 minutes, then garnish with coriander sprigs and serve with rice and lemon wedges.

turkey & aubergine curry

serves 4

- 2 tsp sunflower oil
- 1 onion, chopped
- 2 garlic cloves, crushed
- 1–2 fresh serrano chillies, deseeded and chopped
- 1 tsp ground cumin
- 1 tsp ground coriander
- ½ tsp turmeric
- 1 small aubergine, about 225 g/8 oz, trimmed and cut into small cubes
- 225 g/8 oz skinless, boneless turkey breast, cut into cubes
- 2 carrots, about 175 g/6 oz, peeled and chopped
- 1 small red pepper, deseeded and chopped
- 450 ml/16 fl oz chicken stock
- 1 tbsp chopped fresh coriander, to garnish

1 Heat a wok over a medium heat, then add the oil. Add the onion, garlic and chillies and cook, stirring, for 2 minutes. Sprinkle in all of the spices and cook, stirring constantly, for a further 2 minutes.

2 Add the aubergine and turkey and cook, stirring, for 5 minutes, or until the turkey is browned all over. Add the carrots and red pepper, stir, then pour in the stock. Bring to the boil, cover with a lid and simmer for 20–25 minutes, or until the turkey is tender.

3 Sprinkle with chopped coriander and serve immediately, divided equally between four warmed bowls.

duck jungle curry

serves 4

- 2 tbsp groundnut oil
- 6 tbsp Thai Green Curry Paste (see page 10)
- 1 tbsp finely chopped galangal or ginger root
- 4 tbsp finely chopped shallots
- 2 tbsp fish sauce
- 500 ml/18 fl oz chicken stock
- 350 g/12 oz boneless, skinless duck meat, thinly sliced into small strips
- 150 g/5½ oz baby aubergines, quartered
- 2 small yellow courgettes, thickly sliced diagonally
- 225 g/8 oz can sliced bamboo shoots, drained and rinsed
- juice of 1 lime
- handful of Thai basil leaves
- cooked jasmine rice, to serve

1 Heat a wok over a medium–high heat, then add the oil. Add the curry paste, galangal and shallots and stir-fry for 1 minute until fragrant. Add the fish sauce and stock, and bring to the boil.

2 Add the duck, aubergines and courgettes, and simmer for about 3 minutes until the vegetables have softened slightly. Add the remaining ingredients and simmer for a few more minutes until the duck is tender.

3 Serve immediately in individual bowls, accompanied with rice.

Mmmm...

fish & seafood

balti fish curry

serves 4–6

- 900 g/2 lb thick fish fillets, such as monkfish, grey mullet, cod or haddock, rinsed and cut into large chunks
- 2 bay leaves, torn
- 140 g/5 oz ghee or 150 ml/5 fl oz vegetable oil or groundnut oil
- 2 large onions, chopped
- ½ tbsp salt
- 150 ml/5 fl oz water
- chopped fresh coriander, to garnish
- naan bread, to serve

marinade

- ½ tbsp Garlic and Ginger Paste (see page 11)
- 1 fresh green chilli, deseeded and chopped
- 1 tsp ground coriander
- 1 tsp ground cumin
- ½ tsp ground turmeric
- ¼–½ tsp chilli powder
- 1 tbsp water
- salt

1 To make the marinade, mix the garlic and ginger paste, green chilli, ground coriander, cumin, turmeric and chilli powder together with salt to taste in a large bowl. Gradually stir in the water to form a thin paste. Add the fish chunks and smear with the marinade. Tuck the bay leaves underneath and leave to marinate in the refrigerator for at least 30 minutes, or up to 4 hours.

2 Remove the fish from the refrigerator 15 minutes in advance of cooking. Heat a wok over a medium–high heat, then add the ghee. Add the onions, sprinkle with the salt and cook, stirring frequently, for 8 minutes, or until very soft and golden.

3 Gently add the fish with its marinade and the bay leaves to the wok and stir in the water. Bring to the boil, then immediately reduce the heat and cook the fish for 4–5 minutes, spooning the sauce over the fish and carefully moving the chunks around, until they are cooked through and the flesh flakes easily. Adjust the seasoning, if necessary, then garnish with coriander and serve immediately with naan bread.

fish korma

serves 4

- 700 g/1 lb 9 oz tilapia fillets, cut into 5-cm/2-inch pieces
- 1 tbsp lemon juice
- 1 tsp salt
- 55 g/2 oz cashew nuts
- 3 tbsp sunflower oil
- 5-cm/2-inch piece cinnamon stick, halved
- 4 green cardamom pods, bruised
- 2 cloves
- 1 large onion, finely chopped
- 1–2 fresh green chillies, chopped
- 2 tsp ginger purée
- 2 tsp garlic purée
- 150 ml/5 fl oz single cream
- 55 g/2 oz natural yogurt
- ¼ tsp ground turmeric
- ½ tsp sugar
- 1 tbsp toasted flaked almonds, to garnish
- naan bread, to serve

1 Place the fish on a large plate and gently rub in the lemon juice and ½ teaspoon of the salt. Set aside for 20 minutes. Place the cashew nuts in a heatproof bowl, pour over boiling water and soak for 15 minutes.

2 Heat a wide shallow saucepan over a low heat, then add the oil. Add the cinnamon, cardamom pods and cloves and leave them to sizzle for 30–40 seconds.

3 Add the onion, chillies, ginger purée and garlic purée. Increase the heat slightly and cook, stirring frequently, for 9–10 minutes until the onion is very soft.

4 Meanwhile, drain the cashew nuts and purée them with the cream and yogurt.

5 Stir the turmeric into the onion mixture and add the puréed ingredients, the remaining salt and the sugar. Mix thoroughly and arrange the fish in the sauce in a single layer. Bring to a slow simmer, cover the pan and cook for 5 minutes. Remove the lid and shake the pan gently from side to side. Spoon some of the sauce over the pieces of fish. Re-cover and cook for a further 3–4 minutes. Transfer to a serving dish and garnish with the toasted almonds. Serve immediately with naan bread.

thai green fish curry

serves 4

- 2 tbsp vegetable oil
- 1 garlic clove, chopped
- 2 tbsp Thai Green Curry Paste (see page 10)
- 1 small aubergine, diced
- 125 ml/4 fl oz coconut milk
- 2 tbsp fish sauce
- 1 tsp sugar
- 225 g/8 oz firm white fish fillets, cut into pieces
- 125 ml/4 fl oz fish stock
- 2 kaffir lime leaves, finely shredded
- about 15 fresh Thai basil leaves
- fresh dill sprigs, to garnish

1 Heat a wok over a medium heat, then add the oil and heat until almost smoking. Add the garlic and cook until golden. Add the curry paste and stir-fry for a few seconds before adding the aubergine. Stir-fry for about 4–5 minutes until soft.

2 Add the coconut milk, bring to the boil and stir until it thickens and curdles slightly. Add the fish sauce and sugar to the wok and stir well.

3 Add the fish pieces and stock. Simmer for 3–4 minutes, stirring occasionally, until the fish is just tender. Add the lime leaves and basil, then cook for a further minute. Transfer to a warmed serving dish, then garnish with dill sprigs and serve immediately.

goan fish curry

serves 4

- 4 skinless salmon fillets, about 200 g/7 oz each
- 1 tsp salt, or to taste
- 1 tbsp lemon juice
- 3 tbsp sunflower oil
- 1 large onion, finely chopped
- 2 tsp garlic purée
- 2 tsp ginger purée
- ½ tsp ground turmeric
- 1 tsp ground coriander
- ½ tsp ground cumin
- ½–1 tsp chilli powder
- 250 ml/9 fl oz coconut milk
- 2–3 fresh green chillies, sliced lengthways
- 2 tbsp cider vinegar or white wine vinegar
- 2 tbsp chopped fresh coriander leaves
- cooked basmati rice, to serve

1 Cut each salmon fillet in half and lay on a plate in a single layer. Sprinkle with half the salt and all of the lemon juice and rub in gently. Cover and leave to marinate in the refrigerator for 15–20 minutes.

2 Heat a frying pan over a medium heat, then add the oil. Add the onion and cook, stirring frequently to ensure even colouring, for 8–9 minutes until a pale golden colour.

3 Add the garlic purée and ginger purée and cook, stirring, for 1 minute, then add the turmeric, ground coriander, cumin and chilli powder and cook, stirring, for 1 minute. Add the coconut milk, chillies and vinegar, then add the remaining salt, stir well and simmer, uncovered, for 6–8 minutes.

4 Add the fish and cook gently for 5–6 minutes. Stir in the fresh coriander and remove from the heat. Serve immediately with rice.

bengali-style fish

serves 4–8

- 1 tsp ground turmeric
- 1 tsp salt
- 1 kg/2 lb 4 oz cod fillet, skinned and cut into pieces
- 6 tbsp mustard oil
- 4 fresh green chillies
- 1 tsp finely chopped fresh ginger
- 1 tsp crushed garlic
- 2 onions, finely chopped
- 2 tomatoes, finely chopped
- 450 ml/16 fl oz water
- chopped fresh coriander, to garnish
- naan bread, to serve

1 Mix the turmeric and salt together in a small bowl, then spoon the mixture over the fish pieces.

2 Heat the mustard oil in a large, heavy-based frying pan. Add the fish and fry until pale yellow. Remove the fish with a slotted spoon and reserve.

3 Place the chillies, ginger, garlic, onions and tomatoes in a mortar and grind with a pestle to make a paste. Alternatively, place the ingredients in a food processor and process until smooth.

4 Transfer the spice paste to a clean frying pan and dry-fry until golden brown.

5 Remove the frying pan from the heat and place the fish pieces in the paste without breaking up the fish. Return the frying pan to the heat, add the water and cook over a medium heat for 15–20 minutes. Transfer to a warmed serving dish, garnish with chopped coriander and serve with naan bread.

penang fish curry

serves 4

- 25 g/1 oz dry-roasted peanuts
- 8–10 shallots or 2 onions, roughly chopped
- 2–3 fresh red chillies, roughly chopped
- 2.5-cm/1-inch piece fresh ginger, roughly chopped
- 4 large garlic cloves, roughly chopped
- 1 tsp shrimp paste
- 4 tbsp groundnut oil
- 1 tsp ground turmeric
- ½ tsp chilli powder
- 425 ml/15 fl oz lukewarm water
- ½ tsp salt, or to taste
- 2 tbsp tamarind juice
- ½ tsp sugar
- 700 g/1 lb 9 oz trout fillets, cut into 1-cm/½-inch slices
- fresh coriander sprigs, to garnish
- cooked basmati rice, to serve

1 Put the peanuts, shallots, chillies, ginger, garlic and shrimp paste in a food processor or blender and blend until the mixture is mushy. Remove and set aside.

2 Heat a large, shallow saucepan, preferably non-stick, over a medium heat, then add the oil. Add the peanut mixture, turmeric and chilli powder. Cook, stirring regularly, until the mixture begins to brown, then continue to cook until the mixture is fragrant, adding a little water from time to time to prevent it sticking to the base of the pan. This process will take 10–12 minutes.

3 Pour in the water and add the salt, tamarind juice and sugar. Stir and mix well and carefully add the fish. Stir gently to ensure that the fish is covered with the sauce. Cover the pan, reduce the heat to low and cook for 8–10 minutes. Remove from the heat and serve immediately, garnished with coriander sprigs and accompanied by rice.

fish in coconut

serves 4

- 2 tbsp vegetable or groundnut oil
- 6 spring onions, roughly chopped
- 2.5-cm/1-inch piece fresh ginger, grated
- 2–3 tbsp Thai Red Curry Paste (see page 10)
- 400 ml/14 fl oz coconut milk
- 150 ml/5 fl oz fish stock
- 4 kaffir lime leaves
- 1 lemon grass stalk, broken in half
- 350 g/12 oz white fish fillets, skinned and cut into chunks
- 225 g/8 oz squid rings and tentacles
- 225 g/8 oz large cooked peeled prawns
- 1 tbsp fish sauce
- 2 tbsp Thai soy sauce
- 4 tbsp snipped fresh Chinese chives

1 Heat the oil in a wok or large frying pan and stir-fry the spring onions and ginger for 1–2 minutes. Add the curry paste and stir-fry for 1–2 minutes.

2 Add the coconut milk, fish stock, lime leaves and lemon grass. Bring to the boil, then lower the heat and simmer for 1 minute.

3 Add the fish, squid and prawns and simmer for 2–3 minutes, until the fish is cooked. Add the fish sauce and soy sauce and stir in the chives. Serve immediately.

fish curry

serves 4

- juice of 1 lime
- 4 tbsp Thai fish sauce
- 2 tbsp Thai soy sauce
- 1 fresh red chilli, deseeded and chopped
- 350 g/12 oz monkfish fillet, cut into cubes
- 350 g/12 oz salmon fillet, skinned and cut into cubes
- 400 ml/14 fl oz coconut milk
- 3 kaffir lime leaves
- 1 tbsp Thai Red Curry Paste (see page 10)
- 1 lemon grass stalk (white part only), finely chopped
- 225 g/8 oz jasmine rice, boiled
- 4 tbsp chopped fresh coriander

1 Combine the lime juice, 2 tablespoons of the fish sauce and the soy sauce in a shallow, non-metallic dish. Add the chilli and the fish, stir to coat, cover with clingfilm and chill for 1–2 hours, or overnight.

2 Bring the coconut milk to the boil in a saucepan and add the lime leaves, curry paste, the remaining fish sauce and the lemon grass. Simmer gently for 10–15 minutes.

3 Add the fish and the marinade and simmer gently for 4–5 minutes, until the fish is cooked. Serve hot with freshly cooked rice with chopped coriander stirred through it.

malaysian curry with red snapper

serves 6

- 400 ml/14 fl oz canned coconut milk
- 3 tbsp desiccated coconut
- 2 tbsp groundnut oil
- 2 garlic cloves, finely chopped
- 2 spring onions, thinly sliced
- 2 fresh red chillies, deseeded and finely chopped
- 1 lemon grass stalk, finely chopped
- 2.5-cm/1-inch piece fresh ginger, thinly sliced
- 1 tbsp fish sauce
- 600 ml/1 pint fish or chicken stock
- 1 tbsp sugar
- ¾ tsp ground turmeric
- 2 tbsp lime juice
- 700 g/1 lb 9 oz red snapper fillets, thickly sliced
- salt
- lime wedges, to garnish

1 Pour the coconut milk into a strainer set over a bowl. Heat a wok over a medium–low heat, then add the desiccated coconut and dry-fry, stirring frequently, for 1–2 minutes until lightly browned. Add the oil, garlic, spring onions, chillies, lemon grass and ginger and stir-fry for 3 minutes.

2 Pour the thin coconut milk from the bowl into the wok, reserving the thick coconut milk in the strainer. Stir in the fish sauce, stock, sugar, turmeric and lime juice and season with salt. Bring just to the boil, then reduce the heat and simmer for 10 minutes.

3 Add the pieces of fish and simmer for a further 8–10 minutes until tender. Stir in the reserved coconut milk and simmer for a further 2–3 minutes until thickened. Serve immediately, garnished with lime wedges.

fish tikka

serves 6

- pinch of saffron threads, pounded
- 1 tbsp hot milk
- 85 g/3 oz Greek-style yogurt
- 1 tbsp garlic purée
- 1 tbsp ginger purée
- 1 tsp salt, or to taste
- ½ tsp granulated sugar
- juice of ½ lemon
- ½–1 tsp chilli powder
- ½ tsp garam masala
- 1 tsp ground fennel seeds
- 2 tsp gram flour
- 750 g/1 lb 10 oz salmon fillets, skinned and cut into 5-cm/2-inch cubes
- 3 tbsp olive oil, plus extra for brushing
- sliced tomatoes and cucumber, to garnish
- lemon wedges, to serve

1 Soak the pounded saffron in the hot milk for 10 minutes.

2 Put all the remaining ingredients, except the fish and oil, in a bowl and beat with a fork or a wire whisk until smooth. Stir in the saffron and milk, mix well and add the fish cubes. Using a metal spoon, mix gently, turning the fish around until fully coated with the marinade. Cover and leave to marinate in the refrigerator for 2 hours. Return to room temperature before cooking.

3 Preheat the grill to high. Brush a grill rack generously with oil and 8 metal skewers lightly with oil. Line the grill pan with a piece of foil.

4 Thread the fish cubes onto the prepared skewers, leaving narrow gaps between the pieces. Arrange on the prepared rack and cook under the preheated grill for 3 minutes. Brush half the oil over the kebabs and cook for a further minute. Turn over and brush any remaining marinade over the fish. Cook for 3 minutes. Brush the remaining oil over the fish and cook for a further 2 minutes, or until the fish is lightly charred.

5 Remove from the heat and leave to rest for 5 minutes. Garnish with tomatoes and cucumber and serve with lemon wedges for squeezing over.

cod curry

serves 4

- 1 tbsp vegetable oil
- 1 small onion, chopped
- 2 garlic cloves, chopped
- 2.5-cm/1-inch piece fresh ginger, roughly chopped
- 2 large ripe tomatoes, peeled and roughly chopped
- 150 ml/5 fl oz fish stock
- 1 tbsp medium curry paste
- 1 tsp ground coriander
- 400 g/14 oz canned chickpeas, drained and rinsed
- 750 g/1 lb 10 oz cod fillet, cut into large chunks
- 4 tbsp chopped fresh coriander
- 4 tbsp natural yogurt
- salt and pepper
- cooked basmati rice, to serve

1 Heat a large saucepan over a low heat, then add the oil. Add the onion, garlic and ginger and cook for 4–5 minutes until soft. Remove from the heat. Put the onion mixture into a food processor or blender with the tomatoes and fish stock and process until smooth.

2 Add this mixture to the saucepan with the curry paste, ground coriander and chickpeas. Mix together well, then simmer gently for 15 minutes until thickened.

3 Add the pieces of fish and return to a simmer. Cook for 5 minutes until the fish is just tender. Remove from the heat and leave to stand for 2–3 minutes.

4 Stir in the coriander and yogurt. Season to taste with salt and pepper and serve immediately with rice.

seafood curry

serves 4

- 2 dried red chillies
- 2 tsp coriander seeds
- 1 tsp cumin seed
- 2 cardamom pods
- 1 tsp fenugreek seeds
- 1 tsp black peppercorns
- 1 tsp turmeric
- 1 tsp salt
- 500 g/1 lb 2 oz mixed fillets, e.g. tuna, haddock, mackerel
- 3 tbsp groundnut oil
- 1 large onion, chopped
- 2 garlic cloves, crushed
- 2.5-cm/1-inch piece fresh ginger, finely chopped
- 400 ml/14 fl oz canned coconut milk
- 400 g/14 oz canned chopped plum tomatoes
- 175 g/6 oz raw prawns, peeled and deveined
- chopped fresh coriander, to garnish

1 Place the chillies, coriander seeds, cumin, cardamom, fenugreek and peppercorns in a heavy-based pan and stir on a high heat for 1 minute.

2 Crush the spices finely with a pestle and mortar and add the turmeric and salt.

3 Cut the fish into 5-cm/2-inch chunks and rub with half the spices. Cover and leave to one side.

4 Heat half the oil in a large pan and fry the onion gently for 10 minutes, until soft and golden.

5 Add the garlic, ginger and remaining spices and stir-fry for 1 minute.

6 Make up the coconut milk with water to 500 ml/18 fl oz. Add to the pan with the tomatoes, cover and simmer for 15 minutes.

7 Heat the remaining oil in a frying pan and fry the fish quickly until lightly browned.

8 Add the fish and prawns to the sauce and simmer for 5-6 minutes.

9 Serve the curry immediately, garnished with chopped fresh coriander.

goan-style seafood curry

serves 4–6

- 3 tbsp vegetable or groundnut oil
- 1 tbsp black mustard seeds
- 12 fresh or 1 tbsp dried curry leaves
- 6 shallots, finely chopped
- 1 garlic clove, crushed
- 1 tsp ground turmeric
- ½ tsp ground coriander
- ¼–½ tsp chilli powder
- 140 g/5 oz creamed coconut, grated and dissolved in 300 ml/10 fl oz boiling water
- 500 g/1 lb 2 oz skinless, boneless white fish, such as monkfish or cod, cut into large chunks
- 450 g/1 lb large raw prawns, peeled and deveined
- juice and finely grated rind of 1 lime
- salt
- lime wedges, to serve

1 Heat the oil in a wok or large frying pan over a high heat. Add the mustard seeds and stir them around for about 1 minute, or until they pop. Stir in the curry leaves.

2 Add the shallots and garlic and stir for about 5 minutes, or until the shallots are golden. Stir in the turmeric, coriander and chilli powder and continue stirring for about 30 seconds.

3 Add the dissolved creamed coconut. Bring to the boil, then reduce the heat to medium and stir for about 2 minutes.

4 Reduce the heat to low, add the fish and simmer for 1 minute, spooning the sauce over the fish and very gently stirring it around. Add the prawns and continue to simmer for 4–5 minutes longer until the fish flakes easily and the prawns turn pink and curl.

5 Add half the lime juice, then taste and add more lime juice and salt to taste. Sprinkle with the lime rind and serve with lime wedges.

prawn biryani

serves 8

- 1 tsp saffron strands
- 50 ml/2 fl oz tepid water
- 2 shallots, roughly chopped
- 3 garlic cloves, crushed
- 1 tsp chopped fresh ginger
- 2 tsp coriander seeds
- ½ tsp black peppercorns
- 2 cloves
- seeds from 2 green cardamom pods
- ½ cinnamon stick
- 1 tsp ground turmeric
- 1 green chilli, chopped
- ½ tsp salt
- 2 tbsp ghee
- 1 tsp black mustard seeds
- 500 g/1 lb 2 oz raw tiger prawns, peeled and deveined
- 300 ml/10 fl oz coconut milk
- 300 ml/10 fl oz natural yogurt

to serve/garnish

- freshly cooked rice
- toasted flaked almonds
- sliced spring onion
- sprigs of fresh coriander

1 Soak the saffron in the tepid water for 10 minutes. Put the shallots, garlic, ginger, coriander seeds, peppercorns, cloves, cardamom seeds, cinnamon stick, turmeric, chilli and salt into a spice grinder or mortar and pestle and grind to a paste.

2 Heat the ghee in a saucepan and add the mustard seeds. When they start to pop, add the prawns and stir over a high heat for 1 minute. Stir in the spice mix, then the coconut milk and yogurt. Simmer for 20 minutes.

3 Spoon the prawn mixture into serving bowls. Top with the freshly cooked rice and drizzle over the saffron water. Serve garnished with the flaked almonds, spring onion and sprigs of coriander.

coconut prawns with chillies & curry leaves

serves 4

- 4 tbsp sunflower oil
- ½ tsp black or brown mustard seeds
- ½ tsp fenugreek seeds
- 1 large onion, finely chopped
- 2 tsp garlic purée
- 2 tsp ginger purée
- 1–2 fresh green chillies, chopped
- 1 tbsp ground coriander
- ½ tsp ground turmeric
- ½ tsp chilli powder
- 1 tsp salt, or to taste
- 250 ml/9 fl oz coconut milk
- 450 g/1 lb cooked peeled tiger prawns, thawed if frozen
- 1 tbsp tamarind juice or juice of ½ lime
- ½ tsp crushed black peppercorns
- 10–12 fresh or dried curry leaves

1 Heat a wok over a medium–high heat, then add 3 tablespoons of the oil. When hot, but not smoking, add the mustard seeds, followed by the fenugreek seeds and the onion. Cook, stirring frequently, for 5–6 minutes until the onion is soft but not brown. Add the garlic purée, ginger purée and the chillies and cook, stirring frequently, for a further 5–6 minutes until the onion is a light golden colour.

2 Add the coriander, turmeric and chilli powder and cook, stirring, for 1 minute. Add the salt and coconut milk, followed by the prawns and tamarind juice. Bring to a slow simmer and cook, stirring occasionally, for 3–4 minutes.

3 Meanwhile, heat the remaining oil in a very small saucepan over a medium heat. Add the peppercorns and curry leaves. Turn off the heat and leave to sizzle for 20–25 seconds, then fold the aromatic oil into the prawn mixture. Remove from the heat and serve immediately.

prawn masala

serves 4

- 2 fresh red chillies, deseeded and chopped
- 2 garlic cloves, chopped
- ½ onion, chopped
- 2.5-cm/1-inch piece fresh ginger, chopped
- 1 tsp ground turmeric
- 1 tsp ground cumin
- 1 tsp garam masala
- ½ tsp sugar
- ½ tsp pepper
- 300 ml/10 fl oz natural yogurt
- 2 tbsp chopped fresh coriander
- 500 g/1 lb 2 oz raw tiger prawns, peeled, deveined and tails left intact
- lime wedges, to serve

1 If you are using wooden skewers, soak them in cold water for 30 minutes.

2 Put the chillies into a food processor with the garlic, onion, ginger, turmeric, cumin, garam masala, sugar, pepper and yogurt. Process until smooth, then transfer to a large, shallow dish. Stir in the coriander. Thread the prawns onto metal kebab skewers or pre-soaked wooden skewers, leaving a small space at either end. Transfer them to the dish and turn in the mixture until thoroughly coated. Cover with clingfilm and refrigerate for 1–1½ hours.

3 Preheat the grill. Remove from the refrigerator and arrange the skewers on a grill rack. Cook under a preheated medium grill, turning and basting with the marinade, for 4 minutes, until sizzling and cooked through.

4 Serve hot with lime wedges for squeezing over.

tandoori prawns

serves 4

- 4 tbsp natural yogurt
- 2 fresh green chillies, deseeded and chopped
- ½ tbsp Garlic and Ginger Paste (see page 11)
- seeds from 4 green cardamom pods
- 2 tsp ground cumin
- 1 tsp tomato purée
- ¼ tsp ground turmeric
- ¼ tsp salt
- pinch of chilli powder, ideally Kashmiri chilli powder
- 24 raw tiger prawns, thawed if frozen, peeled, deveined and tails left intact
- oil, for greasing
- lemon or lime wedges, to serve

1 Put the yogurt, chillies and garlic and ginger paste in a spice grinder and blend until a paste forms. Transfer the paste to a large non-metallic bowl and stir in the cardamom pods, cumin, tomato purée, turmeric, salt and chilli powder.

2 Add the prawns to the bowl and, using your hands, coat them with the yogurt marinade. Cover the bowl with clingfilm and chill for at least 30 minutes, or up to 4 hours.

3 When you are ready to cook, heat a large griddle or frying pan over a high heat until a few drops of water 'dance' when they hit the surface. Use crumpled kitchen paper or a pastry brush to grease the hot pan very lightly with oil.

4 Use tongs to lift the prawns out of the marinade, allowing the excess to drip back into the bowl, then place the prawns on the griddle and cook for 2 minutes. Flip them over and cook for a further 1–2 minutes until they turn pink, curl and are opaque all the way through (cut one to test). Serve immediately with lemon or lime wedges for squeezing over.

prawns with spring onions & straw mushrooms

serves 4

- 2 tbsp vegetable or groundnut oil
- bunch of spring onions, chopped
- 2 garlic cloves, finely chopped
- 175 g/6 oz creamed coconut, roughly chopped
- 2 tbsp Thai Red Curry Paste (see page 10)
- 450 ml/16 fl oz fish stock
- 2 tbsp fish sauce
- 2 tbsp Thai soy sauce
- 6 fresh Thai basil sprigs
- 400 g/14 oz canned straw mushrooms, drained
- 350 g/12 oz large cooked peeled prawns
- cooked jasmine rice, to serve

1 Heat the oil in a wok and stir-fry the spring onions and garlic for 2–3 minutes. Add the creamed coconut, curry paste and stock and heat gently until the coconut has dissolved.

2 Stir in the fish sauce and soy sauce, then add the basil, mushrooms and prawns. Gradually bring to the boil and serve immediately with cooked jasmine rice.

mussels in coconut sauce

serves 4

- 1 kg/2 lb 4 oz live mussels, scrubbed and debearded
- 3 tbsp ghee or vegetable oil
- 1 onion, finely chopped
- 1 tsp garlic purée
- 1 tsp ginger purée
- 1 tsp ground cumin
- 1 tsp ground coriander
- ½ tsp ground turmeric
- pinch of salt
- 600 ml/1 pint canned coconut milk
- chopped fresh coriander, to garnish

1 Discard any mussels with broken shells and any that refuse to close when tapped with a knife.

2 Heat a large, heavy-based frying pan over a low heat, then add the ghee. Add the onion and cook, stirring occasionally, for 10 minutes, or until golden.

3 Add the garlic purée and ginger purée and cook, stirring constantly, for 2 minutes. Add the cumin, ground coriander, turmeric and salt and cook, stirring constantly, for a further 2 minutes. Stir in the coconut milk and bring to the boil.

4 Add the mussels, cover and cook for 5 minutes, or until the mussels have opened. Discard any mussels that remain closed. Transfer the mussels, with the coconut sauce, to a large warmed serving dish. Sprinkle with chopped coriander and serve immediately.

mussels with mustard seeds & shallots

serves 4

- 2 kg/4 lb 8 oz live mussels, scrubbed and debearded
- 3 tbsp vegetable oil or groundnut oil
- ½ tbsp black mustard seeds
- 8 shallots, chopped
- 2 garlic cloves, crushed
- 2 tbsp distilled vinegar
- 4 small fresh red chillies
- 85 g/3 oz creamed coconut, dissolved in 300 ml/10 fl oz boiling water
- 10 fresh or 1 tbsp dried curry leaves
- ½ tsp ground turmeric
- ¼–½ tsp chilli powder
- salt

1 Discard any mussels with broken shells or any that refuse to close when tapped with a knife.

2 Heat a wok over a medium–high heat, then add the oil. Add the mustard seeds and stir for about 1 minute, or until they start to pop.

3 Add the shallots and garlic and cook, stirring frequently, for 3 minutes, or until they start to brown. Stir in the vinegar, chillies, creamed coconut, curry leaves, turmeric, chilli powder and a pinch of salt and bring to the boil, stirring.

4 Reduce the heat to very low. Add the mussels, cover the wok and leave the mussels to simmer, shaking the wok frequently, for 3–4 minutes, or until they open. Discard any that remain closed. Ladle the mussels into deep bowls, then taste the broth and add extra salt, if necessary. Spoon the broth over the mussels and serve immediately.

Mmmm...

vegetables & pulses

vegetable korma

serves 4

- 4 tbsp ghee or vegetable oil
- 2 onions, chopped
- 2 garlic cloves, chopped
- 1 fresh red chilli, chopped
- 1 tbsp grated fresh ginger
- 2 tomatoes, peeled and chopped
- 1 orange pepper, deseeded and cut into small pieces
- 1 large potato, cut into chunks
- 200 g/7 oz cauliflower florets
- ½ tsp salt
- 1 tsp ground turmeric
- 1 tsp ground cumin
- 1 tsp ground coriander
- 1 tsp garam masala
- 200 ml/7 fl oz vegetable stock or water
- 150 ml/5 fl oz natural yogurt
- 150 ml/5 fl oz single cream
- 25 g/1 oz fresh coriander, chopped
- freshly cooked rice, to serve

1 Heat the ghee in a large saucepan over a medium heat, add the onions and garlic and cook, stirring, for 3 minutes. Add the chilli and ginger and cook for a further 4 minutes. Add the tomatoes, orange pepper, potato, cauliflower, salt and spices and cook, stirring, for a further 3 minutes. Stir in the stock and bring to the boil. Reduce the heat and simmer for 25 minutes.

2 Stir in the yogurt and cream and cook, stirring, for a further 5 minutes. Add the fresh coriander and heat through. Serve with freshly cooked rice.

vegetables with tofu & spinach

serves 4

- vegetable oil or groundnut oil, for deep-frying, plus 2 tablespoons
- 225 g/8 oz firm tofu, drained and cut into cubes
- 2 onions, chopped
- 2 garlic cloves, chopped
- 1 fresh red chilli, deseeded and sliced
- 3 celery sticks, diagonally sliced
- 225 g/8 oz mushrooms, thickly sliced
- 115 g/4 oz baby corn cobs, cut in half
- 1 red pepper, deseeded and cut into strips
- 3 tbsp Thai Red Curry Paste (see page 10)
- 400 ml/14 fl oz coconut milk
- 1 tsp palm sugar or soft light brown sugar
- 2 tbsp Thai soy sauce
- 225 g/8 oz baby spinach leaves

1 Heat a wok over a high heat, then add the oil for deep-frying and heat to 180–190°C/350–375°F, or until a cube of bread browns in 30 seconds. Add the tofu, in batches, and cook for 4–5 minutes until crisp and brown all over. Remove with a slotted spoon and drain on kitchen paper.

2 Heat a separate wok over a medium heat, then add the 2 tablespoons of oil. Add the onions, garlic and chilli and stir-fry for 1–2 minutes until they start to soften. Add the celery, mushrooms, corn and red pepper and stir-fry for 3–4 minutes until they soften.

3 Stir in the curry paste and coconut milk and gradually bring to the boil. Add the sugar and soy sauce and then the spinach. Cook, stirring constantly, until the spinach has wilted. Serve immediately, topped with the tofu.

spinach & paneer

serves 4

- 85 g/3 oz ghee or 6 tbsp vegetable or groundnut oil
- 350 g/12 oz paneer, cut into 1-cm/½-inch pieces
- 1½ tbsp Garlic and Ginger Paste (see page 11)
- 1 fresh green chilli, chopped
- 4 tbsp water
- 1 onion, finely chopped
- 600 g/1 lb 5 oz fresh spinach leaves, rinsed and any thick stems removed and rinsed
- ¼ tsp salt
- ¼ tsp garam masala
- 4 tbsp double cream
- lemon wedges, to serve

1 Melt the ghee in a flameproof casserole or large frying pan with a tight-fitting lid over a medium–high heat. Add as many paneer pieces as will fit in a single layer without overcrowding the casserole and fry for about 5 minutes until golden brown on all sides. Use a slotted spoon to remove the paneer and drain it on crumpled kitchen paper. Continue, adding a little extra ghee, if necessary, until all the paneer is fried.

2 Put the garlic and ginger paste and chilli in a spice grinder or pestle and mortar and grind until a thick paste forms. Add the water and blend again.

3 Reheat the casserole. Stir in the onion with the garlic and ginger purée mixture and fry, stirring frequently, for 5–8 minutes until the onion is soft, but not brown.

4 Add the spinach, with just the water clinging to the leaves, and the salt, and stir until it wilts. Reduce the heat to low, cover the casserole and continue simmering until the spinach is soft.

5 Stir in the garam masala and cream, then gently return the paneer to the casserole. Simmer, stirring gently, until the paneer is heated through. Taste and adjust the seasoning, if necessary. Serve with lemon wedges for squeezing over.

red curry with mixed leaves

serves 4

- 2 tbsp groundnut oil or vegetable oil
- 2 onions, thinly sliced
- 1 bunch of fine asparagus spears
- 400 ml/14 fl oz coconut milk
- 2 tbsp Thai Red Curry Paste (see page 10)
- 3 fresh kaffir lime leaves
- 225 g/8 oz baby spinach leaves
- 2 heads pak choi, chopped
- 1 small head Chinese leaves, shredded
- handful of fresh coriander, chopped
- cooked jasmine rice, to serve

1 Heat a wok over a medium–high heat, then add the oil. Add the onions and asparagus and stir-fry for 1–2 minutes.

2 Add the coconut milk, curry paste and lime leaves and bring gently to the boil, stirring occasionally. Add the spinach, pak choi and Chinese leaves and cook, stirring, for 2–3 minutes until wilted. Add the coriander and stir well. Serve immediately with rice.

vegetables in a creamy tomato sauce

serves 4

- 200 g/7 oz cauliflower, divided into 1-cm/½-inch florets
- 200 g/7 oz French beans, cut into 5-cm/2-inch lengths
- 200 g/7 oz baby carrots, peeled and left whole
- 200 g/7 oz boiled potatoes
- 4 tbsp sunflower oil
- 5 green cardamom pods, bruised
- 2 bay leaves
- 1 large onion, finely chopped
- 2.5-cm/1-inch piece fresh ginger, finely grated
- 1 tsp ground coriander
- ½ tsp ground cumin
- 1 tsp ground turmeric
- ½–1 tsp chilli powder
- 1 tbsp tomato purée
- 150 ml/5 fl oz lukewarm water
- 150 ml/5 fl oz double cream
- 2 tomatoes, deseeded and roughly chopped
- salt
- naan bread, to serve

1 Bring a saucepan of lightly salted water to the boil and blanch the vegetables, separately (the cauliflower will need 3 minutes, the beans 3 minutes, and the carrots 4 minutes), then drain and plunge in cold water. Cut the potatoes into 2.5-cm/1-inch cubes.

2 Heat a medium-sized saucepan over a low heat, then add the oil. Add the cardamom pods and bay leaves. Allow them to sizzle for 30–40 seconds, then add the onion and ginger. Increase the heat to medium and cook for 5–6 minutes until the onion is soft, stirring regularly.

3 Add the coriander, cumin, turmeric and chilli powder. Cook for 2–3 minutes, then add a little water and continue to cook for a further minute. Add the tomato purée and cook for about a minute.

4 Drain the cauliflower, beans and carrots, and add to the pan along with the potatoes. Add 1 teaspoon of salt, stir and pour in the water. Cook, uncovered, for 2–3 minutes, then add the cream. Cook for 3–4 minutes, then fold in the tomatoes and remove from the heat. Serve immediately with some naan bread.

vegetable sambar

serves 6

- 800 g/1 lb 12 oz canned tomatoes
- 2 tbsp desiccated coconut
- 2 tbsp lemon juice
- 1 tbsp yellow mustard seeds
- 40 g/1½ oz raw or muscovado sugar
- 2 tbsp ghee or vegetable oil
- 2 onions, sliced
- 4 cardamom pods, lightly crushed
- 6 curry leaves, plus extra to garnish
- 2 tsp ground coriander
- 2 tsp ground cumin
- 1 tsp ground turmeric
- 1 tsp ginger purée
- 200 g/7 oz toor dhal
- 450 g/1 lb sweet potatoes, cut into chunks
- 900 g/2 lb potatoes, cut into chunks
- 2 carrots, sliced
- 2 courgettes, cut into chunks
- 1 aubergine, cut into chunks
- salt

1 Place the tomatoes and their can juices, the coconut, 1 tablespoon of the lemon juice, the mustard seeds and sugar in a food processor or blender and process until smooth.

2 Heat the ghee in a large, heavy-based saucepan. Add the onions and cook over a low heat, stirring occasionally, for 10 minutes, or until golden. Add the cardamom pods, curry leaves, coriander, cumin, turmeric and ginger purée and cook, stirring constantly, for 1–2 minutes, or until the spices give off their aroma.

3 Stir in the tomato mixture and dhal and bring to the boil. Reduce the heat, cover and simmer for 10 minutes.

4 Add the sweet potatoes, potatoes and carrots, re-cover the saucepan and simmer for a further 15 minutes. Add the courgettes, aubergine and remaining lemon juice, add salt to taste, re-cover and simmer for a further 10–15 minutes, or until the vegetables are tender. Serve garnished with curry leaves.

okra stir-fried with onions

serves 4

- 280 g/10 oz okra
- 1 small red pepper
- 1 onion
- 2 tbsp sunflower oil
- 1 tsp black or brown mustard seeds
- ½ tsp cumin seeds
- 3 large garlic cloves, lightly crushed, then chopped
- ½ tsp chilli powder
- ½ tsp salt, or to taste
- ½ tsp garam masala
- cooked basmati rice, to serve

1 Scrub each okra gently, rinse well in cold running water, then slice off the hard head. Halve diagonally and set aside.

2 Remove the seeds and core from the red pepper and cut into 4-cm/1-inch strips. Halve the onion lengthways and cut into 5 mm/¼ inch thick slices.

3 Heat a wok over a medium heat, then add the oil. When hot but not smoking, add the mustard seeds, followed by the cumin seeds.

4 Remove from the heat and add the garlic. Return to a low heat and cook the garlic gently, stirring, for 1 minute, or until lightly browned.

5 Add the okra, red pepper and onion, increase the heat to medium–high and stir-fry for 2 minutes. Add the chilli powder and salt and stir-fry for a further 3 minutes. Add the garam masala and stir-fry for 1 minute. Remove from the heat and serve immediately with rice.

vietnamese vegetable curry

serves 6

- 2 lemon grass stalks
- 50 ml/2 fl oz vegetable oil
- 3 large garlic cloves, crushed
- 1 large shallot, thinly sliced
- 2 tbsp Indian curry powder
- 700 ml/1¼ pints coconut milk
- 500 ml/18 fl oz coconut water (not coconut milk) or vegetable stock
- 2 tbsp fish sauce
- 4 fresh red bird's eye chillies or dried red Chinese (tien sien) chillies
- 6 kaffir lime leaves
- 1 carrot, peeled and cut diagonally into 1 cm/½ inch thick pieces
- 1 small-medium Asian aubergine, cut into 2.5-cm/1-inch pieces
- 1 small-medium bamboo shoot, cut into thin wedges
- 115 g/4 oz mangetout, topped and tailed
- 12 large shiitake mushrooms, stems discarded, caps halved
- 450 g/1 lb firm or extra-firm tofu, drained and cut into 2.5-cm/1-inch cubes
- fresh chopped coriander and fried shallots, to garnish

1 Discard the bruised leaves and root ends of the lemon grass stalks, then cut 15–20 cm/6–8 inches of the lower stalks into paper-thin slices.

2 Heat a wok over a high heat, then add the oil. Add the garlic and shallot and stir-fry for 5 minutes, or until golden. Add the lemon grass and curry powder and stir-fry for 2 minutes, or until fragrant.

3 Add the coconut milk, coconut water, fish sauce, chillies and lime leaves and bring to the boil. Reduce the heat to low, then add the carrot and aubergine, cover and cook for 10 minutes.

4 Add the bamboo shoot, mangetout, mushrooms and tofu and cook for a further 5 minutes.

5 Serve immediately, garnished with the coriander and fried shallots.

aubergine & potato curry

serves 4

- 1 large aubergine, about 350 g/12 oz
- 225 g/8 oz potatoes, boiled in their skins and cooled
- 3 tbsp sunflower oil
- ½ tsp black mustard seeds
- ½ tsp nigella seeds
- ½ tsp fennel seeds
- 1 onion, finely chopped
- 2.5-cm/1-inch piece fresh ginger, grated
- 2 fresh green chillies, chopped
- ½ tsp ground cumin
- 1 tsp ground coriander
- 1 tsp ground turmeric
- ½ tsp chilli powder
- 1 tbsp tomato purée
- 450 ml/16 fl oz lukewarm water
- 1 tsp salt, or to taste
- ½ tsp garam masala
- 2 tbsp chopped fresh coriander leaves
- naan bread, to serve

1 Quarter the aubergine lengthways and cut the stem end of each quarter into 5-cm/2-inch pieces. Halve the remaining part of each quarter and cut into the same size as above. Soak the aubergine pieces in cold water.

2 Peel the potatoes and cut into 5-cm/2-inch cubes. Heat a large saucepan over a medium heat, then add the oil. When hot, add the mustard seeds and, as soon as they start popping, add the nigella seeds and fennel seeds. Add the onion, ginger and chillies and cook for 7–8 minutes until the mixture begins to brown.

3 Add the cumin, ground coriander, turmeric and chilli powder. Cook for about a minute, then add the tomato purée. Cook for a further minute, pour in the water, then add the salt and aubergine. Bring to the boil and cook over a medium heat for 8–10 minutes, stirring frequently to ensure that the aubergine cooks evenly. At the start of cooking, the aubergine will float, but once it soaks up the liquid it will sink quickly. As soon as this happens, add the potatoes and cook for 2–3 minutes, stirring.

4 Stir in the garam masala and chopped coriander and remove from the heat. Serve immediately with naan bread.

mushrooms in a rich tomato & onion sauce

serves 4

- 280 g/10 oz closed cup white mushrooms
- 4 tbsp sunflower or olive oil
- 1 onion, finely chopped
- 1 green chilli, finely chopped
- 2 tsp garlic purée
- 1 tsp ground cumin
- 1 tsp ground coriander
- ½ tsp chilli powder
- ½ tsp salt, or to taste
- 1 tbsp tomato purée
- 3 tbsp water
- 1 tbsp snipped fresh chives

1 Wipe the mushrooms with damp kitchen paper and slice thickly.

2 Heat the oil in a medium-sized saucepan over a medium heat. Add the onion and chilli and cook, stirring frequently, for 5–6 minutes, until the onion is soft but not brown. Add the garlic purée and cook, stirring, for 2 minutes.

3 Add the cumin, coriander and chilli powder and cook, stirring, for 1 minute. Add the mushrooms, salt and tomato purée and stir until all the ingredients are thoroughly blended.

4 Sprinkle the water evenly over the mushrooms and reduce the heat to low. Cover and cook for 10 minutes, stirring halfway through. The sauce should have thickened, but if it appears runny, cook, uncovered, for 3–4 minutes, or until you achieve the desired consistency.

5 Transfer to a serving dish, sprinkle with the chives and serve immediately.

spiced black-eyed beans & mushrooms

serves 4

- 1 onion, roughly chopped
- 4 large garlic cloves, roughly chopped
- 2.5-cm/1-inch piece fresh ginger, roughly chopped
- 4 tbsp sunflower oil
- 1 tsp ground cumin
- 1 tsp ground coriander
- ½ tsp ground fennel
- 1 tsp ground turmeric
- ½–1 tsp chilli powder
- 175 g/6 oz canned chopped tomatoes
- 400 g/14 oz canned black-eyed beans, drained and rinsed
- 115 g/4 oz large flat mushrooms, wiped and cut into bite-sized pieces
- ½ tsp salt, or to taste
- 175 ml/6 fl oz lukewarm water
- 1 tbsp chopped fresh mint
- 1 tbsp chopped fresh coriander leaves
- naan bread, to serve

1 Purée the onion, garlic and ginger in a food processor or blender.

2 Heat a medium-sized saucepan over a medium heat, then add the oil. Add the puréed ingredients and cook for 4–5 minutes, then add the cumin, ground coriander, ground fennel, turmeric and chilli powder. Stir-fry for about a minute, then add the tomatoes. Cook until the tomatoes are pulpy and the juice has evaporated.

3 Add the black-eyed beans, mushrooms and salt. Stir well and pour in the water, bring to the boil, cover the pan and reduce the heat to low. Simmer for 8–10 minutes, stirring halfway through.

4 Stir in the chopped mint and coriander and remove from the heat. Transfer to a serving dish and serve with naan bread.

paneer in chilli-tomato sauce

serves 4

- 4 tbsp sunflower or olive oil
- 250 g/9 oz paneer, cut into 2.5-cm/1-inch cubes
- 4 green cardamom pods, bruised
- 2 bay leaves
- 1 onion, finely chopped
- 2 tsp garlic purée
- 2 tsp ginger purée
- 2 tsp ground coriander
- ½ tsp ground turmeric
- ½–1 tsp chilli powder
- 150 g/5½ oz canned chopped tomatoes
- 450 ml/16 fl oz warm water
- 1 tsp salt, or to taste
- 125 g/4½ oz frozen peas
- ½ tsp garam masala
- 2 tbsp single cream
- 2 tbsp chopped fresh coriander leaves

1 Heat 2 tablespoons of the oil in a medium non-stick saucepan over a medium heat. Add the paneer and cook, stirring frequently, for 3–4 minutes, or until evenly browned. Paneer tends to splatter in hot oil, so be careful. Remove and drain on kitchen paper.

2 Add the remaining oil to the saucepan and reduce the heat to low. Add the cardamom pods and bay leaves and allow to sizzle gently for 20–25 seconds. Add the onion, increase the heat to medium and cook, stirring frequently, for 4–5 minutes, until the onion is soft. Add the garlic and ginger purées and cook, stirring frequently, for a further 3–4 minutes, until the onion is a pale golden colour.

3 Add the ground coriander, turmeric and chilli powder and cook, stirring, for 1 minute. Add the tomatoes and cook, stirring, for 4–5 minutes. Add 2 tablespoons of the warm water and cook, stirring, for 3 minutes, or until the oil separates from the spice paste.

4 Add the remaining warm water and the salt. Bring to the boil, then reduce the heat to low and simmer, uncovered, for 7–8 minutes. Add the paneer and peas and simmer for 5 minutes. Stir in the garam masala, cream and fresh coriander and remove from the heat. Serve immediately.

lentils with cumin & shallots

serves 4

- 200 g/7 oz red split lentils (masoor dhal)
- 850 ml/1½ pints water
- 1 tsp salt, or to taste
- 2 tsp sunflower oil
- ½ tsp black or brown mustard seeds
- ½ tsp cumin seeds
- 4 shallots, finely chopped
- 2 fresh green chillies, chopped
- 1 tsp ground turmeric
- 1 tsp ground cumin
- 1 fresh tomato, chopped
- 2 tbsp chopped fresh coriander leaves

1 Wash the lentils until the water runs clear and put into a medium-sized saucepan. Add the water and bring to the boil. Reduce the heat to medium and skim off the foam. Cook, uncovered, for 10 minutes. Reduce the heat to low, cover and cook for 45 minutes, stirring occasionally to ensure that the lentils do not stick to the base of the pan as they thicken. Stir in the salt.

2 Meanwhile, heat a small saucepan over a medium heat, then add the oil. When hot, but not smoking, add the mustard seeds, followed by the cumin seeds. Add the shallots and chillies and cook, stirring, for 2–3 minutes, then add the ground turmeric and cumin. Add the tomato and cook, stirring, for 30 seconds.

3 Fold the shallot mixture into the cooked lentils. Stir in the coriander, remove from the heat and serve immediately.

mixed lentils with five-spice seasoning

serves 4

- 125 g/4½ oz red split lentils (masoor dhal)
- 125 g/4½ oz skinless split mung beans (mung dhal)
- 850 ml/1½ pints hot water
- 1 tsp ground turmeric
- 1 tsp salt, or to taste
- 1 tbsp lemon juice
- 2 tbsp sunflower oil
- ¼ tsp black mustard seeds
- ¼ tsp cumin seeds
- ¼ tsp nigella seeds
- ¼ tsp fennel seeds
- 4–5 fenugreek seeds
- 2–3 dried red chillies
- 1 small tomato, deseeded and cut into strips, and fresh coriander sprigs, to garnish
- naan bread, to serve

1 Mix the lentils and beans together and wash until the water runs clear. Put them into a large saucepan with the hot water. Bring to the boil and reduce the heat slightly. Leave to boil for 5–6 minutes and, when the foam subsides, add the turmeric, reduce the heat to low, cover and cook for 20 minutes. Add the salt and lemon juice and beat the dhal with a wire whisk. Add a little more hot water if the dhal is too thick.

2 Heat a small saucepan over a medium heat, then add the oil. When hot, but not smoking, add the mustard seeds. As soon as they begin to pop, reduce the heat to low and add the cumin seeds, nigella seeds, fennel seeds, fenugreek seeds and chillies. Leave the spices to sizzle until the seeds begin to pop and the chillies have blackened. Pour the contents of the saucepan over the lentils, scraping every bit out of the saucepan.

3 Turn off the heat and keep the lentils covered until you are ready to serve. Transfer to a serving dish and garnish with tomato strips and coriander sprigs. Serve hot with naan bread.

lentils with fresh chillies, mint & coriander

serves 4

- 85 g/3 oz red split lentils (masoor dhal)
- 85 g/3 oz skinless split chickpeas (channa dhal)
- 3 tbsp sunflower oil
- 1 onion, finely chopped
- 2–3 fresh green chillies, chopped
- 2 tsp garlic purée
- 2 tsp ginger purée
- 1 tsp ground cumin
- 600 ml/1 pint lukewarm water
- 1 tsp salt, or to taste
- 1 tbsp chopped fresh mint
- 1 tbsp chopped fresh coriander leaves
- 55 g/2 oz unsalted butter
- 1 fresh green chilli and 1 small tomato, deseeded and cut into julienne strips, to garnish

1 Wash the lentils and chickpeas together until the water runs clear and leave to soak for 30 minutes.

2 Heat a medium-sized saucepan, preferably non-stick, over a medium heat, then add the oil. Add the onion, chillies, garlic purée and ginger purée. Stir-fry the mixture until it begins to brown.

3 Drain the lentils and chickpeas and add to the onion mixture together with the cumin. Reduce the heat to low and stir-fry for 2–3 minutes, then pour in the water. Bring to the boil, reduce the heat to low, cover and simmer for 25–30 minutes.

4 Stir in the salt, mint, coriander and butter. Stir until the butter has melted, then remove from the heat. Serve hot, garnished with chilli and tomato strips.

carrot & pumpkin curry

serves 4

- 150 ml/5 fl oz vegetable stock
- 2.5-cm/1-inch piece fresh galangal, sliced
- 2 garlic cloves, chopped
- 1 lemon grass stalk (white part only), finely chopped
- 2 fresh red chillies, deseeded and chopped
- 4 carrots, peeled and cut into chunks
- 225 g/8 oz pumpkin, peeled, deseeded and cut into cubes
- 2 tbsp vegetable or groundnut oil
- 2 shallots, finely chopped
- 3 tbsp Thai Yellow Curry Paste (see page 10)
- 400 ml/14 fl oz coconut milk
- 4–6 fresh Thai basil sprigs
- 25 g/1 oz toasted pumpkin seeds, to garnish

1 Pour the stock into a large saucepan and bring to the boil. Add the galangal, half the garlic, the lemon grass and chillies and simmer for 5 minutes. Add the carrots and pumpkin and simmer for 5–6 minutes, until tender.

2 Meanwhile, heat the oil in a wok or frying pan and stir-fry the shallots and the remaining garlic for 2–3 minutes. Add the curry paste and stir-fry for 1–2 minutes.

3 Stir the shallot mixture into the saucepan and add the coconut milk and Thai basil. Simmer for 2–3 minutes. Serve hot, sprinkled with the toasted pumpkin seeds.

cauliflower & sweet potato curry

serves 4

- 4 tbsp ghee or vegetable oil
- 2 onions, finely chopped
- 1 tsp panch phoran
- 1 cauliflower, broken into small florets
- 350 g/12 oz sweet potatoes, diced
- 2 fresh green chillies, deseeded and finely chopped
- 1 tsp ginger paste
- 2 tsp paprika
- 1½ tsp ground cumin
- 1 tsp ground turmeric
- ½ tsp chilli powder
- 3 tomatoes, quartered
- 225 g/8 oz fresh or frozen peas
- 3 tbsp natural yogurt
- 225 ml/8 fl oz vegetable stock or water
- 1 tsp garam masala
- salt
- sprigs of fresh coriander, to garnish

1 Heat the ghee in a large, heavy-based frying pan. Add the onions and panch phoran and cook over a low heat, stirring frequently, for 10 minutes, or until the onions are golden. Add the cauliflower, sweet potatoes and chillies and cook, stirring frequently, for 3 minutes.

2 Stir in the ginger paste, paprika, cumin, turmeric and chilli powder and cook, stirring constantly, for 3 minutes. Add the tomatoes and peas and stir in the yogurt and stock. Season with salt to taste, cover and simmer for 20 minutes, or until the vegetables are tender.

3 Sprinkle the garam masala over the curry, transfer to a warmed serving dish and serve immediately, garnished with sprigs of fresh coriander.

green bean & potato curry

serves 6

- 300 ml/10 fl oz vegetable oil
- 1 tsp white cumin seeds
- 1 tsp mixed mustard and onion seeds
- 4 dried red chillies
- 3 fresh tomatoes, sliced
- 1 tsp salt
- 1 tsp finely chopped fresh ginger
- 1 tsp crushed fresh garlic
- 1 tsp chilli powder
- 200 g/7 oz green beans, diagonally sliced into 2.5-cm/1-inch lengths
- 2 potatoes, peeled and diced
- 300 ml/10 fl oz water
- chopped fresh coriander and finely sliced green chillies, to garnish

1 Heat the oil in a large heavy-based saucepan. Add the white cumin seeds, mustard and onion seeds and dried red chillies, stirring well.

2 Add the tomatoes to the pan and stir-fry the mixture for 3–5 minutes.

3 Mix the salt, ginger, garlic and chilli powder together in a bowl and spoon into the saucepan. Blend the whole mixture together.

4 Add the green beans and potatoes to the saucepan and stir-fry for 5 minutes.

5 Add the water to the saucepan, reduce the heat and simmer for 10–15 minutes, stirring occasionally. Transfer to a warmed serving dish, garnish with chopped coriander and green chillies and serve.

chickpeas in coconut milk

serves 4–6

- 275 g/9¾ oz potatoes, cut into 1-cm/½-inch cubes
- 250 ml/9 fl oz hot water
- 400 g/14 oz canned chickpeas, drained and rinsed
- 250 ml/9 fl oz coconut milk
- 1 tsp salt, or to taste
- 2 tbsp sunflower oil
- 4 large garlic cloves, finely chopped or crushed
- 2 tsp ground coriander
- ½ tsp ground turmeric
- ½–1 tsp chilli powder
- juice of ½ lemon
- cooked basmati rice, to serve

1 Put the potatoes in a medium saucepan and pour in the hot water. Bring to the boil, then reduce the heat to low and cook, covered, for 6–7 minutes. Add the chickpeas and cook, uncovered, for 3–4 minutes, until the potatoes are tender.

2 Add the coconut milk and salt and bring to a slow simmer. Meanwhile, heat the oil in a small saucepan over a low heat. Add the garlic and cook, stirring frequently, until it begins to brown. Add the coriander, turmeric and chilli powder and cook, stirring, for 25–30 seconds.

3 Fold the aromatic oil into the chickpeas. Stir in the lemon juice and remove from the heat. Serve immediately with cooked basmati rice.

chickpea curry

serves 4

- 6 tbsp vegetable oil
- 2 onions, sliced
- 1 tsp finely chopped fresh ginger
- 1 tsp ground cumin
- 1 tsp ground coriander
- 1 tsp crushed fresh garlic
- 1 tsp chilli powder
- 2 fresh green chillies, finely chopped
- 2–3 tbsp fresh coriander leaves
- 150 ml/5 fl oz water
- 1 large potato
- 400 g/14 oz canned chickpeas, drained
- 1 tbsp lemon juice

1 Heat the oil in a large, heavy-based saucepan. Add the onions and cook, stirring occasionally, until golden. Reduce the heat, add the ginger, ground cumin, ground coriander, garlic, chilli powder, green chillies and coriander leaves and stir-fry for 2 minutes.

2 Add the water to the mixture in the saucepan and stir to mix.

3 Using a sharp knife, cut the potato into dice, then add with the chickpeas to the saucepan. Cover and leave to simmer, stirring occasionally, for 5–7 minutes.

4 Sprinkle the lemon juice over the curry. Transfer to serving dishes and serve hot.

Mmmm...
accompaniments

onion bhajis

serves 4

- 150 g/5½ oz gram flour
- 1 tsp salt, or to taste
- small pinch of bicarbonate of soda
- 25 g/1 oz ground rice
- 1 tsp fennel seeds
- 1 tsp cumin seeds
- 2 green chillies, finely chopped
- 2 large onions, about 400 g/14 oz, sliced into half-rings and separated
- 15 g/½ oz fresh coriander, including the tender stalks, finely chopped
- 200 ml/7 fl oz water
- sunflower oil, for deep-frying
- Mango Chutney (see page 216) or tomato chutney, to serve

1 Sift the gram flour into a large bowl and add the salt, bicarbonate of soda, ground rice, fennel seeds and cumin seeds. Mix together thoroughly, then add the chillies, onions and coriander. Gradually pour in the water and mix until a thick batter has formed and all the other ingredients are thoroughly coated with it.

2 Heat a wok over a high heat, then add the oil and heat to 180–190°C/350–375°F, or until a cube of bread browns in 30 seconds. If the oil is not hot enough, the bhajis will be soggy. Add as many ½ tablespoons of the batter as will fit in a single layer, without overcrowding.

3 Reduce the heat slightly and cook the bhajis for 8–10 minutes until golden brown and crisp. Maintaining a steady temperature is important to ensure that the centres of the bhajis are cooked, while the outsides turn brown. Remove and drain on kitchen paper. Keep hot in a low oven while you cook the remaining batter. Serve hot with chutney.

vegetable samosas

makes 12

- 3 tbsp sunflower or olive oil
- ½ tsp black mustard seeds
- 1 tsp cumin seeds
- 1 tsp fennel seeds
- 1 onion, finely chopped
- 2 green chillies, finely chopped
- 2 tsp ginger purée
- ½ tsp ground turmeric
- 1 tsp ground coriander
- 1 tsp ground cumin
- ½ tsp chilli powder
- 350 g/12 oz boiled potatoes, cut into bite-sized pieces
- 125 g/4½ oz frozen peas, thawed
- 1 tsp salt, or to taste
- 2 tbsp chopped fresh coriander leaves
- 12 sheets filo pastry, about 28 x 18 cm/11 x 7 inches
- 55 g/2 oz butter, melted, plus extra for greasing
- chutney, to serve

1 Heat the oil in a saucepan over a medium heat and add the mustard seeds, followed by the cumin and fennel seeds. Then add the onion, chillies and ginger purée and cook, stirring frequently, for 5–6 minutes, until the onion is soft but not brown.

2 Add the spices and cook, stirring, for 1 minute. Add the potatoes, peas and salt and stir until the vegetables are thoroughly coated with the spices. Stir in the coriander and remove from the heat. Leave to cool completely.

3 Preheat the oven to 180°C/350°F/Gas Mark 4 and line a baking sheet with baking paper. Place a sheet of filo pastry on a board and brush well with the melted butter. Keep the remaining pastry sheets covered with clingfilm. Fold the buttered pastry sheet in half lengthways, brush with some more melted butter and fold lengthways again.

4 Place about 1 tablespoon of the vegetable filling on the bottom right-hand corner of the pastry sheet and fold over to form a triangle. Continue folding to the top of the sheet, maintaining the triangular shape, and moisten the ends to seal the edges. Transfer to the prepared baking sheet and brush with melted butter. Repeat with the remaining sheets of filo pastry and filling.

5 Bake the samosas in the preheated oven for 20 minutes. Serve hot with chutney.

bombay potatoes

serves 6

- 500 g/1 lb 2 oz new potatoes, diced
- 1 tsp ground turmeric
- pinch of salt
- 4 tbsp ghee or vegetable oil
- 6 curry leaves
- 1 dried red chilli
- 2 fresh green chillies, chopped
- ½ tsp nigella seeds
- 1 tsp mixed mustard and onion seeds
- ½ tsp cumin seeds
- ½ tsp fennel seeds
- ¼ tsp asafoetida
- 2 onions, chopped
- 5 tbsp chopped fresh coriander
- juice of ½ lime

1 Place the potatoes in a large, heavy-based saucepan and pour in just enough cold water to cover. Add ½ teaspoon of the turmeric and the salt and bring to the boil. Simmer for 10 minutes, or until tender, then drain and reserve until required.

2 Heat a large, heavy-based frying pan over a medium–high heat, then add the ghee. Add the curry leaves and dried red chilli and cook, stirring frequently, for a few minutes, or until the chilli is blackened. Add the remaining turmeric, the fresh chillies, the nigella seeds, mixed mustard and onion seeds, cumin seeds, fennel seeds, asafoetida, onions and coriander and cook, stirring constantly, for 5 minutes, or until the onions have softened.

3 Add the potatoes, stir and cook over a low heat, stirring frequently, for 10 minutes, or until the potatoes have heated through. Squeeze over the lime juice and serve immediately.

sag aloo

serves 4

- 500 g/1 lb 2 oz fresh spinach leaves
- 2 tbsp ghee or vegetable oil
- 1 tsp black mustard seeds
- 1 onion, halved and sliced
- 2 tsp Garlic and Ginger paste (see page 11)
- 900 g/2 lb waxy potatoes, cut into small chunks
- 1 tsp chilli powder
- 125 ml/4 fl oz vegetable stock or water
- salt

1 Bring a large saucepan of water to the boil. Add the spinach leaves and blanch for 4 minutes. Drain well, then tip into a clean tea towel, roll up and squeeze out the excess liquid.

2 Heat the ghee in a separate saucepan. Add the mustard seeds and cook over a low heat, stirring constantly, for 2 minutes, or until they give off their aroma. Add the onion, and garlic and ginger paste and cook, stirring frequently, for 5 minutes, or until softened.

3 Add the potatoes, chilli powder and stock and season to taste with salt. Bring to the boil, cover and cook for 10 minutes. Add the spinach and stir it in, then cover and simmer for a further 10 minutes, or until the potatoes are tender. Serve immediately.

aloo gobi

serves 4–6

- 55 g/2 oz ghee or 4 tbsp vegetable or groundnut oil
- ½ tbsp cumin seeds
- 1 onion, chopped
- 4-cm/1½-inch piece fresh ginger, finely chopped
- 1 fresh green chilli, deseeded and thinly sliced
- 450 g/1 lb cauliflower, cut into small florets
- 450 g/1 lb large waxy potatoes, peeled and cut into large chunks
- ½ tsp ground coriander
- ½ tsp garam masala
- ¼ tsp salt
- fresh coriander sprigs, to garnish

1 Heat the ghee in a flameproof casserole or large frying pan with a tight-fitting lid over a medium–high heat. Add the cumin seeds and stir around for about 30 seconds until they crackle and start to brown.

2 Immediately stir in the onion, ginger and chilli and stir for 5–8 minutes until the onion is golden.

3 Stir in the cauliflower and potatoes, followed by the ground coriander, garam masala and salt, and continue stirring for about 30 seconds longer.

4 Cover the pan, reduce the heat to the lowest setting and simmer, stirring occasionally, for 20–30 minutes until the vegetables are tender when pierced with the point of a knife. Check occasionally that they aren't sticking to the base of the pan and stir in a little water, if necessary.

5 Serve garnished with sprigs of coriander.

pilau rice

serves 2–4

- 200 g/7 oz basmati rice
- 2 tbsp ghee
- 3 green cardamom pods
- 2 whole cloves
- 3 black peppercorns
- ½ tsp salt
- ½ tsp saffron threads
- 400 ml/14 fl oz water

1 Rinse the rice in several changes of water until the water runs clear, then leave to soak for 30 minutes. Drain and set aside until ready to cook.

2 Heat a heavy-based saucepan over a medium–high heat, then add the ghee. Add the cardamom pods, cloves and peppercorns and stir-fry for 1 minute. Add the rice and stir-fry for a further 2 minutes.

3 Add the salt, saffron and water to the rice mixture and reduce the heat. Cover the saucepan and leave to simmer over a low heat for 20 minutes until all the water has evaporated.

4 Transfer the rice to a large, warmed serving dish and serve hot.

coconut rice

serves 4–6

- 225 g/8 oz basmati rice
- 450 ml/16 fl oz water
- 60 g/2¼ oz creamed coconut
- 2 tbsp mustard oil
- 1½ tsp salt

1 Rinse the basmati rice in several changes of water until the water runs clear, then leave to soak for 30 minutes. Drain and set aside until ready to cook.

2 Bring the water to the boil in a small saucepan, stir in the creamed coconut until it dissolves and then set aside.

3 Heat the mustard oil in a large frying pan or saucepan with a lid over a high heat until it smokes. Turn off the heat and leave the mustard oil to cool completely.

4 When you are ready to cook, reheat the mustard oil over a medium–high heat. Add the rice and stir until all the grains are coated in oil. Add the water with the dissolved coconut and bring to the boil.

5 Reduce the heat to its lowest setting, stir in the salt and cover the pan tightly. Simmer, without lifting the lid, for 8–10 minutes, until the grains are tender and all the liquid is absorbed.

6 Turn off the heat and use 2 forks to mix the rice. Adjust the seasoning, if necessary. Re-cover the pan and leave the rice to stand for 5 minutes.

lemon-laced basmati rice

serves 4

- 225 g/8 oz basmati rice
- 2 tbsp sunflower oil
- ½ tsp black or brown mustard seeds
- 10–12 curry leaves, preferably fresh
- 25 g/1 oz cashew nuts
- ¼ tsp ground turmeric
- 1 tsp salt, or to taste
- 450 ml/16 fl oz hot water
- 2 tbsp lemon juice

1 Wash the rice in several changes of cold water until the water runs clear. Leave to soak in fresh cold water for 20 minutes, then leave to drain in a colander.

2 Heat a non-stick saucepan over a medium heat, then add the oil. When hot, but not smoking, add the mustard seeds, followed by the curry leaves and the cashew nuts.

3 Stir in the turmeric, quickly followed by the rice and salt. Cook, stirring, for 1 minute, then add the hot water and lemon juice. Stir once, bring to the boil and boil for 2 minutes. Cover tightly, reduce the heat to very low and cook for 8 minutes. Turn off the heat and leave to stand, covered, for 6–7 minutes. Fork through the rice and transfer to a serving dish. Serve immediately.

spiced basmati pilau

serves 4

- 500 g/1 lb 2 oz basmati rice
- 175 g/6 oz broccoli, trimmed
- 6 tbsp vegetable oil
- 2 large onions, chopped
- 225 g/8 oz mushrooms, sliced
- 2 garlic cloves, crushed
- 6 cardamom pods, split
- 6 whole cloves
- 8 black peppercorns
- 1 cinnamon stick or piece of cassia bark
- 1 tsp ground turmeric
- 1.2 litres/2 pints vegetable stock or water
- 55 g/2 oz seedless raisins
- 55 g/2 oz unsalted pistachios, roughly chopped
- salt and pepper

1 Place the rice in a sieve and wash well under cold running water. Drain. Trim off most of the broccoli stalk and cut the head into small florets, then quarter the stalk lengthways and cut diagonally into 1-cm/½-inch pieces.

2 Heat the oil in a large saucepan. Add the onions and broccoli stalks and cook over a low heat, stirring frequently, for 3 minutes. Add the mushrooms, rice, garlic and spices and cook for 1 minute, stirring, until the rice is coated in oil.

3 Add the stock and season to taste with salt and pepper. Stir in the broccoli florets and return the mixture to the boil. Cover, reduce the heat and cook over a low heat for 15 minutes without uncovering the pan.

4 Remove the pan from the heat and leave the pilau to stand for 5 minutes without uncovering. Remove the whole spices, add the raisins and pistachios and gently fork through to fluff up the grains. Serve the pilau hot.

naan bread

makes 3

- 280 g/10 oz strong white flour, plus extra for dusting
- 1 tsp salt
- 1 tbsp ground coriander
- 1 garlic clove, very finely chopped
- 1 tsp easy-blend dried yeast
- 2 tsp clear honey
- 100 ml/3½ fl oz lukewarm water
- 4 tbsp natural yogurt
- 1 tbsp vegetable oil, plus extra for brushing
- 1 tsp black onion seeds
- 1 tbsp chopped fresh coriander

1 Sift the flour, salt and ground coriander together into a bowl and stir in the garlic and yeast. Make a well in the centre and pour in the honey, water, yogurt and oil. Stir well until the dough begins to come together, then knead with your hands until it leaves the side of the bowl. Turn out onto a lightly floured surface and knead well for about 10 minutes, until smooth and elastic. Brush a bowl with oil. Shape the dough into a ball, put it in the bowl and cover with a damp tea towel. Leave to rise in a warm place for 1–2 hours, until the dough has doubled in volume.

2 Put three baking trays in the oven and preheat to 240°C/475°F/Gas Mark 9. Preheat the grill. Turn out the dough onto a lightly floured surface and knock back with your fist. Divide the dough into three pieces, shape each piece into a ball and cover two of them with oiled clingfilm. Roll out the uncovered piece of dough into a teardrop shape about 8 mm/⅜ inch thick and cover with oiled clingfilm. Roll out the other pieces of dough in the same way. Place the naan on the preheated baking trays and sprinkle with the onion seeds and chopped coriander. Bake in the preheated oven for 5 minutes, until puffed up. Transfer the naan bread to the grill pan, brush with oil and grill for 2–3 minutes. Serve warm.

chapattis

makes 16

- 400 g/14 oz chapatti flour (atta), plus extra for dusting
- 1 tsp salt
- ½ tsp granulated sugar
- 2 tbsp sunflower oil
- 250 ml/9 fl oz lukewarm water

1 Mix the flour, salt and sugar together in a large bowl. Add the oil and work well into the flour mixture with your fingertips. Gradually add the water, mixing at the same time. When the dough is formed, transfer to a work surface and knead for 4–5 minutes. The dough is ready when all the excess moisture has been absorbed by the flour. Alternatively, mix the dough in a food processor. Wrap the dough in clingfilm and leave to rest for 30 minutes.

2 Divide the dough in half, then cut each half into eight equal-sized pieces. Form each piece into a ball and flatten into a round cake. Dust each cake lightly in flour and roll out to a 15-cm/6-inch round. Keep the remaining cakes covered while you are working on one. The chapattis will cook better when freshly rolled out, so roll them out and cook them one at a time.

3 Heat a heavy-based cast-iron griddle or a large, heavy-based frying pan over a medium–high heat. Put a chapatti on the griddle and cook for 30 seconds. Using a fish slice, turn it over and cook until bubbles begin to appear on the surface. Turn it over again. Press the edges down gently with a clean cloth to encourage the chapatti to puff up – they will not always puff up, but this doesn't matter. Cook until brown patches appear on the underside. Remove from the pan and keep hot by wrapping in a piece of foil lined with kitchen paper. Repeat with the remaining chapattis. Serve warm.

pooris

makes 12

- 225 g/8 oz wholemeal flour, sifted, plus extra for dusting
- ½ tsp salt
- 25 g/1 oz ghee, melted
- 100–150 ml/3½–5 fl oz water
- vegetable oil or groundnut oil, for deep-frying

1 Put the flour and salt into a bowl and drizzle the ghee over the surface. Gradually stir in the water until a stiff dough forms.

2 Turn out the dough onto a lightly floured work surface and knead for 10 minutes, or until it is smooth and elastic. Shape the dough into a ball and place it in the cleaned bowl, then cover with a damp tea towel and leave to rest for 20 minutes.

3 Divide the dough into 12 equal-sized pieces and roll each into a ball. Working with one ball of dough at a time, flatten the dough between your palms, then thinly roll it out on a lightly floured work surface into a 13-cm/5-inch round. Continue until all the dough balls are rolled out.

4 Heat a wok over high heat, then add oil to a depth of at least 7.5 cm/3 inches and heat until it reaches 180–190°C/350–375°F, or until a cube of bread browns in 30 seconds. Drop one poori into the hot fat and fry for about 10 seconds, or until it puffs up. Use two large spoons to flip the poori over and spoon some hot oil over the top.

5 Use the two spoons to lift the poori from the oil and allow any excess oil to drip back into the wok. Drain the poori on crumpled kitchen paper and serve immediately. Continue until all the pooris are fried, making sure the oil returns to the correct temperature before you add another poori. Serve warm.

dosas

makes 8

- 115 g/4 oz basmati rice, rinsed
- 70 g/2½ oz split black lentils (urad dal chilke)
- ¼ tsp fenugreek seeds
- 125 ml/4 fl oz water
- 25 g/1 oz ghee, melted
- salt

1 Bring a saucepan of lightly salted water to the boil, add the rice and boil for 5 minutes, then drain. Put the rice, lentils and fenugreek seeds in a bowl with water to cover and leave to soak overnight.

2 Strain the rice and lentils, reserving the soaking liquid. Put the rice and lentils in a food processor with 75 ml/2½ fl oz of the water and process until smooth. Slowly add the remaining water. Cover the bowl with a damp tea towel and leave to ferment in a warm place for 5–6 hours.

3 Stir the mixture and add as much extra water as necessary to get a consistency of single cream. Add salt to taste.

4 Heat a large frying pan over a high heat until a splash of water 'dances' when it hits the surface, then brush the surface with melted ghee. Put a ladleful of batter in the centre of the pan and use the base of the ladle to spread it out as thinly as possible, then leave it to cook for 2 minutes until it is golden brown and crisp on the base.

5 Flip the dosa over and continue cooking for a further 2 minutes. Turn it out of the pan and continue cooking until all the batter has been used. Serve warm or cold.

plantain chips

serves 4

- 4 ripe plantains
- 1 tsp mild, medium or hot curry powder, to taste
- vegetable or groundnut oil, for deep-frying
- mango chutney, to serve

1 Peel the plantains, then cut crossways into 3-mm/⅛-inch slices. Put the slices in a bowl, sprinkle over the curry powder and use your hands to lightly toss together.

2 Heat enough oil for deep-frying in a wok, deep-fat fryer or large heavy-based saucepan to 180°C/350°F, or until a cube of bread browns in 30 seconds. Add as many plantain slices as will fit in the pan without overcrowding and fry for 2 minutes, or until golden.

3 Remove the plantain chips from the pan with a slotted spoon and drain well on crumpled kitchen paper. Serve hot with mango chutney.

cucumber raita

serves 4–5

- 1 small cucumber
- 175 g/6 oz natural yogurt
- ¼ tsp granulated sugar
- ¼ tsp salt
- 1 tsp cumin seeds
- 10–12 black peppercorns
- ¼ tsp paprika

1 Peel the cucumber and scoop out the seeds. Cut the flesh into bite-sized pieces and set aside.

2 Put the yogurt into a bowl and beat with a fork until smooth. Add the sugar and salt and mix well.

3 Heat a small, heavy-based saucepan over a medium–high heat. When the pan is hot, turn off the heat and add the cumin seeds and peppercorns. Stir for 40–50 seconds, until they release their aroma.

4 Remove from the pan and leave to cool for 5 minutes, then crush in a mortar with a pestle or on a hard surface with a rolling pin.

5 Reserve ¼ teaspoon of this mixture and stir the remainder into the yogurt. Add the cucumber and stir to mix. Transfer the raita to a serving dish and sprinkle with the reserved toasted spices and the paprika.

chilli & onion chutney

makes 225 g/8 oz

- 1–2 fresh green chillies, finely chopped
- 1 small fresh bird's eye chilli, finely chopped
- 1 tbsp white wine vinegar or cider vinegar
- 2 onions, finely chopped
- 2 tbsp fresh lemon juice
- 1 tbsp sugar
- 3 tbsp chopped fresh coriander, mint or parsley, or a combination of herbs
- salt
- chilli flower, to garnish

1 Put the chillies in a small non-metallic bowl with the vinegar, stir and then drain. Return the chillies to the bowl and stir in the onions, lemon juice, sugar and herbs, then add salt to taste.

2 Leave to stand at room temperature or cover and chill for 15 minutes. Garnish with the chilli flower before serving.

coconut sambal

makes about 140 g/5 oz

- ½ fresh coconut or 125 g/4½ oz desiccated coconut
- 2 fresh green chillies, deseeded or not, to taste, and chopped
- 2.5-cm/1-inch piece fresh ginger, peeled and finely chopped
- 4 tbsp chopped fresh coriander
- 2 tbsp lemon juice, or to taste
- 2 shallots, very finely chopped

1 If you are using a whole coconut, use a hammer and nail to punch a hole in the 'eye' of the coconut, then pour out the water from the inside and reserve. Use the hammer to break the coconut in half, then peel half and chop.

2 Put the coconut and chillies in a food processor and process for about 30 seconds until finely chopped. Add the ginger, coriander and lemon juice and process again.

3 If the mixture seems too dry, stir in about 1 tablespoon of coconut water or water. Stir in the shallots and serve immediately, or cover and chill until required. This will keep its fresh flavour in the refrigerator for up to 3 days.

mango chutney

makes 250 g/9 oz

- 1 large mango, about 400 g/14 oz, peeled, stoned and finely chopped
- 2 tbsp lime juice
- 1 tbsp vegetable oil or groundnut oil
- 2 shallots, finely chopped
- 1 garlic clove, finely chopped
- 2 fresh green chillies, deseeded and finely sliced
- 1 tsp black mustard seeds
- 1 tsp coriander seeds
- 5 tbsp palm sugar or soft light brown sugar
- 5 tbsp white wine vinegar
- 1 tsp salt
- pinch of ground ginger

1 Put the mango in a non-metallic bowl with the lime juice and set aside.

2 Heat a large frying pan or saucepan over a medium–high heat, then add the oil. Add the shallots and cook for 3 minutes. Add the garlic and chillies and stir for a further 2 minutes, or until the shallots are soft but not brown. Add the mustard seeds and coriander seeds and stir.

3 Add the mango to the pan with the sugar, vinegar, salt and ginger and stir. Reduce the heat to its lowest setting and simmer for 10 minutes until the liquid thickens and the mango becomes sticky.

4 Remove from the heat and leave to cool completely. Transfer to an airtight container, then cover and chill for 3 days before using.

lime pickle

serves 6–8

- 12 limes, halved and deseeded
- 115 g/4 oz salt
- 70 g/2½ oz chilli powder
- 25 g/1 oz mustard powder
- 25 g/1 oz ground fenugreek
- 1 tbsp ground turmeric
- 300 ml/10 fl oz mustard oil
- 15 g/½ oz yellow mustard seeds, crushed
- ½ tsp asafoetida

1 Cut each lime half into 4 pieces and pack them into a large sterilized jar, sprinkling over the salt at the same time. Cover and leave to stand in a warm place for 10–14 days, or until the limes have turned brown and softened.

2 Mix together the chilli powder, mustard powder, fenugreek and turmeric in a small bowl and add to the jar of limes. Stir to mix, then re-cover and leave to stand for 2 days.

3 Transfer the lime mixture to a heatproof bowl. Heat the mustard oil in a heavy-based frying pan. Add the mustard seeds and asafoetida to the pan and cook, stirring constantly, until the oil is very hot and just beginning to smoke.

4 Pour the oil and spices over the limes and mix well. Cover and leave to cool. When cool, pack into a sterilized jar, seal and store in a sunny place for 1 week before serving.

coriander chutney

serves 4–5

- 1½ tbsp lemon juice
- 1½ tbsp water
- 85 g/3 oz fresh coriander leaves and stems, roughly chopped
- 2 tbsp chopped fresh coconut
- 1 small shallot, very finely chopped
- 5-mm/¼-inch piece fresh ginger, chopped
- 1 fresh green chilli, deseeded and chopped
- ½ tsp sugar
- ½ tsp salt
- pinch of pepper

1 Put the lemon juice and water in a small food processor, add half the coriander and process until it is blended and a slushy paste forms. Gradually add the remaining coriander and process until it is all blended, scraping down the sides of the processor, if necessary.

2 If you don't have a processor that will cope with this small amount, use a pestle and mortar, adding the coriander in small amounts.

3 Add the remaining ingredients and continue processing until they are all finely chopped and blended. Taste and adjust the seasonings, if necessary. Transfer to a non-metallic bowl, cover and chill for up to 3 days before serving.

Index